D0870226

Toward a Strategy for Urban Integration

LESSONS IN
SCHOOL AND HOUSING POLICY
FROM TWELVE CITIES

by Gary Orfield

A REPORT TO THE FORD FOUNDATION

One of a series of reports on activities supported by the
Ford Foundation. A complete list of publications may be
obtained from the Ford Foundation, Office of Reports,
320 East 43 Street, New York, New York 10017.

Library of Congress Cataloging in Publication Data

Orfield, Gary.
  Toward a strategy for urban integration.

  1. School integration—United States—Case studies.
2. Discrimination in housing—Government policy—United
States—Case studies. 3. Education, Urban—United
States—Case studies. 4. Race discrimination—United
States—Case studies. 5. United States—Race relations
—Case studies. I. Ford Foundation. II. Title.
LC212.5.073   370.19'342   81-19447
ISBN 0-916584-19-4   AACR2

Contents

Preface

Racial segregation by public policy in the country's schools was declared unconstitutional in the Supreme Court's 1954 decision in *Brown* v *Board of Education*. Desegregation of the schools has been a requirement of the federal courts since then. In 1964 the Civil Rights Act was passed, stipulating in Title VI that no federal funds could flow to any agency practicing discrimination on the basis of race, religion, or national origin. The Civil Rights Act was followed a year later by the Elementary and Secondary Education Act (ESEA), which provided significant federal funds for schools. Because of Title VI, the federal executive branch became responsible for determining whether discrimination existed in the school districts receiving federal funds.

Federal policies outlawing racial segregation in housing came later. Even though the Federal Housing Administration had by 1948 abandoned its overtly segregationist policies with respect to the siting of public housing, practices changed slowly. The first corrective measure was an Executive Order issued by President Kennedy in 1962 making discrimination unlawful in housing owned or financed by the federal government. The Civil Rights Act of 1964 imposed a blanket ban on discrimination "under any program or activity receiving federal financial assistance." Fair housing finally became the law of the land, covering private as well as publicly financed housing, with the passage of the Civil Rights Act of 1968 and the Supreme Court's ruling in *Jones* v *Mayer* the same year that housing discrimination is prohibited by the Thirteenth Amendment as a vestige of slavery.

These measures have thus far had only a modest impact on residential segregation by race. First, they are not self-enforcing. They have been invoked with neither sufficient regularity nor severe enough sanctions to have the kind of deterrent effect necessary to change institutional practices. An effort in Congress in 1980 to strengthen the enforcement provisions of the Civil Rights Act failed. Second, housing differs from schools in that its occupancy is controlled not by duly constituted public authorities but by the private decisions of many individual home seekers operating in a highly fragmented housing market.

The primary evidence of discrimination in the schools for both the courts and the executive branch was the racial segregation of students and faculty. Since 1965 the courts, the Department of Health, Education and Welfare (HEW) (now Health and Human Services), and more recently the Department of Education have struggled to define remedies for segregated schools. Most of the problems dealt with in this long, difficult, and unfinished task have required altering patterns of school attendance and the assignment of teachers. The purpose has been to reduce racial isolation in the schools by seeking some degree of integration of the races.

The federal courts had no idea how to desegregate schools when the Supreme Court in 1954 ordered that it be brought about "with all deliberate speed," and the executive branch had no experience in the field when it joined the courts in working on desegregation in 1965 as a result of the duties conferred on it by the combination of Title VI of the Civil Rights Act and ESEA. School districts were no better off and were inclined to do nothing until the courts or the executive branch set requirements for them.

Over the last fifteen years or more, numerous strategies have developed for desegregating schools. Magnet schools have been created to attract pupils of both races; attendance lines within school districts have been redrawn to reduce racial isolation; and teacher assignment policies have been revised. The first priority in putting these and other strategies into operation was understandably to deal with discrimination in states that had enacted laws requiring segregation of the races in schools under the "separate but equal" doctrine to which the Supreme Court had given approval until 1954. These were the states of the South, where an elaborate system of busing had for years carried youngsters to "white schools" and "black schools." It is not surprising, therefore, that busing students to desegregated schools became a major policy instrument of the judicial and executive branches in dealing with racial discrimination in those states.

In the 1960s only a few steps were taken by the courts and the executive branch to address the problems of discriminatory segregation in states where no law had required a dual system of officially designated black and white schools. But starting in the late 1960s and with growing momentum through the 1970s, the school districts of Northern states (and particularly those of cities

with large concentrations of racial minorities) were required by
the courts and by HEW to establish desegregation plans. Many
strategies were used in these plans, but almost all of them
required some transportation of students by bus to offset the patterns of racial assignment growing out of the typical housing patterns in Northern cities. In those cities blacks and Hispanics gen-
erally lived in federally financed and slum housing; they lived
apart from whites and attended schools that included few if any
whites. In these places little or nothing could be done about racial
isolation in the schools without substantial busing. Indeed, the
racial concentrations were so great in some cities that little could
be done with busing unless the courts were willing to order school
districts outside the central city to exchange students with it.

The main observation that can be made about busing to desegregate the schools is that it is unpopular. Civil rights advocates
and minority groups support busing as the only available means to
achieve integration in residentially segregated cities. Many people
find it inconvenient and would much prefer to live in integrated
neighborhoods within which youngsters could attend neighborhood schools. Such views raise the question of why racial
minorities have been forced to live in segregated enclaves and
what might be done about that fact by considering housing policy
along with school desegregation policy.

The concentration of racial minorities in American cities did
not happen by accident. Discrimination in the sale, rental, and
financing of housing in the private market along with the central-
city location of much public and publicly assisted housing helped
sharpen the color lines of city living. The Ford Foundation has for
fifteen years supported efforts of voluntary organizations to promote minority access to housing throughout metropolitan areas.
These efforts include locating new subsidized housing in the suburbs as well as inducing the gatekeepers to open up the existing
market. The new-construction approach produced some impres-
sive court victories but little suburban integration. Nevertheless,
minorities have moved to the suburbs in substantial numbers over
the past decade. Although we do not yet know how many of these
moves constitute resegregation and how many genuine integration, the growth of minority representation in the suburbs offers
an opportunity for further progress in desegregating metropolitan America if the existing markets continue to open up.

Against this background the Ford Foundation started four
years ago to explore the possibilities of considering housing
segregation and school segregation as related matters. We wanted

to see whether courts could deal with both at the same time and whether housing agencies and school officials could work together to promote long-term planning about both, which might ultimately reduce the need for busing. The results of these explorations were published in 1979 in two reports to the Ford Foundation, collectively entitled *Racial Segregation: Two Policy Views*, by Gary Orfield and William Taylor. Their reports developed some of the conceptual possibilities for dealing with housing and school segregation simultaneously and addressed some of the legal aspects as well.

This document is the second the Foundation has issued on the subject. To prepare it, Gary Orfield looked carefully at local situations that might benefit from combined attention to housing and schools in seeking solutions to problems of discrimination. (Among other things, he noted that in many places the officials who deal with one area are unknown to those in the other and take actions without regard to effects on the other.) Professor Orfield offers no panacea, but he does identify considerable potential for making progress toward a desegregated society by trying to work on issues of school and housing segregation together. He makes a series of suggestions for joint activity that offer hope toward the resolution of one of our country's most frustrating dilemmas.

HAROLD HOWE II
Vice President for Education and Public Policy

FORD FOUNDATION
May 1981

Introduction

Perhaps the most difficult test of public leadership is honestly facing and effectively attacking problems that pose fundamental long-term threats to our society but require short-term changes that are intensely unpopular. Racial segregation is such a threat. Faced with extraordinary challenges, the easiest short-term course is to ignore the issue or join the popular attack on the difficult solutions. It is all too easy to justify such conduct with any number of arguments—perhaps the long-term menace will not materialize; perhaps it will be impossible to act until the public changes its mind; the duty of leaders is to reflect public opinion whatever it is; probably the well-intentioned policies will never work anyway, and many others.

The peculiar quality of strong leadership is the capacity to see the fundamental problems that must be addressed and to find strategies that will increase the chance of reaching solutions. One part of such leadership is to perceive very painful but inevitable changes not only as difficulties but also as opportunities. The momentum of change can be used to carry thought and action along to more basic, long-term reforms, or it can be allowed to dissipate in confusion and recriminations.

Urban school desegregation is a basic social and educational change. Almost always it is imposed on a community that steadfastly refuses to act on its own. Usually it is done with little or no local planning. As time passes the issue dies away and a new status quo of desegregated schools emerges. Too often, however, the school plan is operated without imagination or timely revision and resegregation occurs. Though citizens often comment that busing is an artificial way to get at a problem caused by housing segregation, there is rarely any initiative on housing. Sometimes the nature or the administration of the school plan, or both, even increases the problem of residential separation.

I began this study with the simple conviction that there must be a better way, and the hope that local officials had worked out some of the answers. I began it with the realization, expressed in an earlier report to the Ford Foundation (Orfield and Taylor, *Racial Segregation: Two Policy Views*, 1979), that the federal government had no coherent urban desegregation policy or strategy. My hope was that some local governments had learned how to do successfully what most have not wished to do at all; that some knew how to plan for a future most prefer to pretend will not arrive. Sharing my hope that it is not too late to turn toward an integrated society in our metropolitan areas, and my conviction that to do nothing is to choose segregation, Ford Foundation officials supported my search for models across the U.S. In the great cities of Ohio, most of which are in the midst of school desegregation struggles, similar work was carried out by Dr. Rachel Tompkins of the Citizens' Council for Ohio Schools.

COMMUNITIES INVESTIGATED

This study was designed to search for models of coordination, not to examine a cross section of American communities. Therefore, I limited it to communities that have school desegregation plans, that are experiencing relatively little community conflict over the issue, and that (in most cases) have reputations for relatively progressive local leadership on racial issues. I left out communities that retain highly segregated schools and communities that have already resegregated and have virtually all-minority school districts. Serious consideration of long-term policy alternatives is most likely where doing something cannot be avoided and where there appears to be some possibility of long-term success in stabilizing integration.

I studied five communities with metropolitan school desegregation plans,* four with plans only for the central city in metropolitan areas that had a relatively small minority population, one suburb with a long-time record of commitment to school and housing integration, and two Big Ten university centers with records of early action against discrimination. (Much of the early school desegregation outside the South occurred during the mid-1960s in

---

*Metropolitan desegregation plans include much if not all of the area of continuous urbanization in a metropolitan community. A metropolitan plan may result either from the full desegregation of a single school district that contains the metropolitan community—as in many of the large countywide school districts of Florida—or through the imposition of a court-ordered plan that merges (and thereby desegregates) previously independent city and suburban school districts or requires the reassignment of students among districts that retain their separate existence.

university communities.) The communities, visited in late 1979 or early 1980, are:

Charlotte–Mecklenburg, N.C.
(the first metropolitan desegregation order, 1971)
Pinellas County, Fla.
(metropolitan St. Petersburg)
New Castle County, Del.
(a metropolitan plan merging separate metropolitan Wilmington school districts, 1978)
Jefferson County, Ky.
(the first metropolitan merger plan; Louisville and suburban county system, 1975)
Leon County, Fla.
(metropolitan Tallahassee)
Seattle, Wash.
(the nation's only voluntarily adopted large-city desegregation plan using mandatory busing)
Milwaukee, Wis.
(the nation's most successful big-city plan relying primarily on magnet schools)
Minneapolis, Minn.
(a big-city plan in a district with relatively few black students; implemented with considerable school-district support)
Denver, Colo.
(the first big-city Supreme Court order for desegregation in the North, 1973; a metropolitan area with a relatively small minority population)
Ann Arbor, Mich.
(University of Michigan college town; partial desegregation plan)
Champaign–Urbana, Ill.
(University of Illinois college towns; districtwide desegregation plans in 1966)
Teaneck, N.J.
(a New York City suburb; one of the first involuntary plans with busing in the U.S., 1964)

I held discussions with a wide range of policy makers and experts in each city selected. I always included talks with officials from the school district and the city government. I also interviewed housing officials, community development administrators, regional planners, local urban policy experts, and civil rights leaders or administrators of civil rights agencies.

The information on which this study is based was supplemented by my study of Chicago suburbs facing racial change, and by information from Los Angeles, Phoenix, Houston, Omaha, St. Louis, Chicago, and other cities. The findings of Dr. Rachel Tompkins' Ohio study were very helpful as were published materials and government documents from individual cities.

The experience of short and very intense visits to a wide variety of communities was fascinating. With few exceptions, local officials were very willing to discuss the issues, and many were greatly interested in the experience of other cities. Active controversies and community struggle over the busing issue had long since died away in most of the cities. Many of the school administrators were doing fine work in trying to build high-quality integrated schools, with little real help. No large city had made a substantial commitment to housing integration, but all had officials who were acutely aware of and concerned about the persistent forces of ghetto creation and barrio expansion in their areas. In several communities a small number of people—who typically lived in integrated neighborhoods themselves—were deeply committed to developing policies for an integrated society. I came home with the conviction that, given the appropriate information and some policy guidance and support from other levels of government, communities can devise much better and more successful long-term strategies. The task should not be delayed.

Coordinated Integration Strategies: Assumptions and Findings

If any cities had rational and coordinated approaches to urban integration, I assumed for this project, they would be those that had already passed through the most controversial test—school desegregation—and emerged in relatively good condition. Just as you could reasonably expect to find the best practice of preventive medicine among heart-disease patients who had undergone difficult surgery because of their past failings, you could expect a community whose public school system had been fundamentally altered by findings of local violations to be aware of the segregation problem and the advantages of a long-range, locally designed integration policy.

Among white Americans the constituency for any kind of desegregation initiative is very small. Surveys in recent years have consistently shown that a low priority is assigned to racial issues and that among whites there is a strong belief that enough has already been done for blacks and Hispanics.[1] Also, many minority persons either reject desegregation or give it a low priority. It is not surprising, therefore, to find that nothing much is done about a city's housing integration as long as the racial issue can be ignored altogether. Once a desegregation order imposes a busing system on a city, however, changes occur. If you were to ask a cross section of local leaders, in cities that lived through school controversies, whether they would prefer a policy that would eventually integrate schools naturally, their support would probably be unanimous. It is only logical to assume that policies for integrated housing would be seen in a different light once racial change was inevitable. It might even be possible to promote it as a better alternative to the existing system.[2] A big city with an exemplary housing integration program is very likely to be a city that previously had an extensive busing order.

More than a quarter century after the decision of the U.S. Supreme Court in *Brown* v *Board of Education of Topeka* and almost a decade after the first urban busing case, you would hope that some city had leaders who had devised a practical way to combine intelligently planned school integration, skillfully implemented policies to create and maintain integrated neighborhoods, and supportive attacks on job discrimination. Everyone, including the judges, agreed that the courts should not run major urban institutions if there were any alternatives. There were capable local officials who had detailed knowledge of their communities and responsibility for many programs that could assist or impede integration. Somewhere in the U.S., then, there should be constructive experiments to observe. We know of cities that have failed spectacularly in dealing with the school desegregation challenge and cities that have managed very well indeed. This study attempted to find communities that had taken the next step beyond, a step toward mobilizing diverse local and locally administered resources to build integration, even as they were mobilized to create and expand segregation.

SUMMARY OF FINDINGS

Among the cities studied there is no fully developed policy for integration, but various approaches have been used with positive effect. Local officials were not opposed to development of pro-integration policies, but many did not feel it was their responsibility. Usually the issue had not been discussed among local agencies or between local and federal authorities. Although school officials were universally in favor of help from housing programs, very few had taken any concrete step to get that help. This was the pattern that emerged:

1) In cities with large-scale mandatory school desegregation, there is virtually unanimous support among officials for the proposition that school and housing desegregation should be coordinated. This proposition is most strongly supported by school officials. Action on the housing issue by school boards or administrators rarely goes beyond disparaging comments, wistful hopes, and toothless resolutions.

2) Actual coordination is virtually nonexistent.

3) Officials in school and housing agencies do not understand each other's programs and plans and rarely make effective use of each other's data.

4) Those who could most easily point out the need for coordinated action—elected city officials and planners constantly studying local urban trends—tend to avoid any discussion of integration issues, fearing controversy.

5) Most school desegregation plans and orders are designed without strong incentives for action on the housing issues. Some may actually discourage it.

6) In most cities, neither school nor housing authorities have systematically studied the existing integrated neighborhoods or devised policies to stabilize them.

7) Local officials report receiving neither policies nor encouragement from federal agencies for coordination of school and housing desegregation strategies.

8) To the extent that there has been an effort to modify the earlier, segregated patterns of subsidized housing, it has concentrated on economic rather than racial desegregation. The common assumption has been that if subsidized housing is built in white suburbs, integration will automatically occur. This is incorrect.

9) Few cities have organized professional programs to help middle-class minority families move into white areas.

10) Some assume that natural integration of urban schools will come out of the urban revitalization process that is bringing back middle-class whites to some central-city neighborhoods. Data show, however, that the overall return rate is rather low and has very little, if any, impact on school enrollment now. There are policies, however, that might help the trend to further school integration.

11) Solutions for parts of the problem have been found in several of the cities studied—positive approaches by local leaders, courts, civil rights leaders, housing officials, and others.

12) Officials usually asked for ideas developed elsewhere, and expressed strong interest in initiating local discussion.

Like any other survey, this study can only summarize what exists now. Many of the discussions, however, gave a good deal of attention to what could be done. Almost all officials believed that improvements could be made, in some instances with only modest effort.

If It's Such a Good Idea, Why Doesn't Anyone Do It?

Perhaps the most disconcerting aspect of this search for a coordinated school and housing policy is that everyone says it would be a good idea but almost no one does anything about it. An obvious, and apparently reasonable, way to reconcile this inconsistency would be to conclude that people don't really mean what they say. Political and administrative leaders often affirm values they do not act on. No doubt there is an element of hypocrisy here.

More basic explanations are available, however. Local officials do not know how to run a coordinated policy—which is understandable since it has never been done—and they confront barriers of divided power and weak interagency relationships. A coordinated policy would mean shifting some of the responsibility for integration from officials who have been at the center of the battle (the school authorities) to others who have remained largely uninvolved (the city housing and community development authorities and the federal Department of Housing and Urban Development). Few officials or agencies borrow problems, particularly in areas where the methods and the long-term rewards are not yet clear. Most prefer to continue operating in traditional fashion and to ignore the damage they do to the policies of other agencies or to the long-term future of the urban community.

The extent of the mutual ignorance among officials is astonishing. When housing offices evaluated the likely racial impact of decisions on locations for subsidized housing in early 1980, they relied on racial statistics for census tracts from the 1970 census. None of the housing, community development, or planning officials interviewed—except in Charlotte, N.C.—made explicit use of school racial statistics in reaching housing decisions. Racial statistics a decade old are often almost useless in rapidly changing cities. Statistics on census tracts, which refer to large areas, may show little or nothing about what is happening at the neighborhood level, the level where integration or racial transition actually occurs.

Up-to-date statistics on racial change at the neighborhood level would be much more valuable. Many officials with responsibilities for housing decisions don't even know that school districts report enrollment statistics by race for every neighborhood public school every year. Very few use these data, which cover the period from the late 1960s to the present and show a great deal about trends in segregation, integration, and transition in neighborhoods. They are the best available information on neighborhood racial change and provide an essential tool for a sensible integration policy.

HOW TO MEASURE IMPACT

The information needed to initially assess the impact of a proposed housing action on school desegregation is relatively simple to describe. You need to know the race and location of those benefiting from various housing programs serving families (units for the elderly and one-bedroom units don't affect schools), the residential racial composition of the neighborhood public school students, and the nature of the school desegregation plan. For a more complete assessment, it is important to know whether the racial composition of the local school population is stable or changing, the racial composition of those on local waiting lists for subsidized housing, and the process by which tenants are selected.

With this information it would be relatively easy to assess the impact of any housing action or program. Information in this form was not available in any of the cities I visited or in any other community I have studied.

All housing and city-government officials interviewed in cities with large-scale school desegregation plans are aware of the existence of a plan, but almost none has any detailed information about the way the plan works. After discussing a pending housing action, which could well have the unintended consequence of increasing school segregation and disrupting a significant portion of the metropolitan Louisville plan, the housing director of the local HUD office observed that perhaps he should have a map of the school plan in his office.[3] Even so simple a tool could call attention to some of the difficulties caused by totally uncoordinated actions. No housing official interviewed could say even how many of the tenants in local subsidized housing lived in integrated or segregated neighborhoods. Obviously they could not answer questions about the impact of their programs on the schools.

In most school districts the only official consulted regularly about housing development decisions is the one responsible for facilities planning. When a new subdivision or subsidized project is on the drawing board, the planners often ask the school district whether the local school has enough classroom space to accommodate the children. Since most urban school districts now have a great deal of extra space, this is seldom a serious problem.

Unfortunately, the facilities planner has nothing to do with the desegregation staff, and he is not asked to report on the implications of housing construction for school segregation. No one in the school district is asked this question. The school district is simply expected to cope with whatever is done to it.

WHY NO ONE ASKS THE CRUCIAL QUESTIONS

One of the most striking features of discussion with local officials is the widespread understanding that racial issues are very important in urban development. This understanding is shared by many people who nonetheless carry on their work as if racial issues were insignificant or nonexistent. In most planning offices, for example, there is no significant analysis, prepared or in process, on local residential-integration patterns, though many planners have personal knowledge of the subject. Planners tend to ignore school questions in general and school integration questions in particular, yet most concede that these were very important factors in attracting and holding middle-class families in the city. School problems in general and school racial problems in particular are important public concerns according to surveys of several cities.[4] Because the issues were politically controversial, they were simply left out of planning work, although they were widely viewed as crucial by the very officials who ignored them.

A few planners are concentrating specifically on stabilizing integration, working principally in what I call mobilized suburbs. These are communities, directly in the path of expanding ghettos, that have decided to use all aspects of local governmental authority to attempt to preserve integration. Planning for integration is particularly evident in parts of the Chicago and Cleveland suburbs where some towns have achieved stable and substantial integration. In such communities, planning for integration is seen as a vital civic necessity, the only alternative to inclusion in a growing ghetto.[5] No big cities have programs of this kind.

On any aspect of school desegregation, the record of elected city officials is usually dismal. They actively criticize the school district and attack the busing plan, but make no connection at all between the controversy and housing decisions. With the striking exception of the mobilized suburbs and a few central-city neighborhood organizations struggling for stability, there is very little discussion of housing integration as a policy and even less of the connection between housing and school integration.[6] Where there is no specific attention to the problem, the usual pattern is continuation of housing practices that actually increase school segregation. Cities with delicately balanced school desegregation plans are often earnestly pursuing housing policies that are unintentionally but steadily undermining the school plan.

The record is full of missed opportunities. In Minneapolis, for example, the public housing authority was willing to come under a judicial injunction prohibiting future site selections that would increase segregation. The local school-board attorney, however, delayed filing of papers on the issue for years. By the time school officials did file, the housing authority had changed its mind; it successfully argued that the action had been taken too late in the development of the school case.[7] In Louisville, the federal judge rejected an effort to bring housing authorities into the school case.[8] In the Coney Island case in New York City, the court ordered a housing remedy but then reversed itself.[9] St. Louis litigation in 1980 brought the first order for development of federal and local housing policies to support school integration.[10]

In many school desegregation cases evidence on intentional housing segregation is introduced as part of the proof of local violations. How, the court is asked, can neighborhood schools be continued if government policy sees to it that the neighborhoods themselves are segregated? An important part of the proof of interdistrict violations in the Wilmington and Indianapolis cases concerned public housing violations.[11] School systems' lawyers often argue that the blame for segregated schools should really be placed on housing officials not on the school district.[12]

COURT ORDERS AND INCENTIVES FOR ACTION ON HOUSING

Although housing issues are much discussed in school desegregation cases, and although desegregation plans must overcome the effects of housing violations as well as intentional school segregation, no attention is normally given to housing issues in the design and implementation of the remedy. Housing policies cause part of the problem of segregated schools, but they are not required to produce part of the solution.

School cases outside the South are usually divided into two phases. First, there is a protracted and complex battle to prove constitutional violation. Once it is shown that local decisions contributed substantially to school segregation, the Supreme Court requires that all segregation within the school system be presumed to be unconstitutional unless shown otherwise and that it be remedied to the greatest extent. Virtually all urban school districts that are sued are eventually found guilty.

The remedy stage that follows is typically shorter and is largely limited to a contest over the design of a student reassignment plan. If the school district designs a plan that meets the goal of the court, it is usually ordered into effect. The court will usually approve any plan designed by local school authorities that assigns both white and minority children to schools integrated at the required level. If the school district refuses to develop such a plan, a method of reassigning students may be taken from plans drawn by experts hired by the civil rights litigants, or the judge himself may formulate the plan. Often it does not even mention housing.

The desegregation plan is drawn by school officials, a planner, or a judge who ordinarily knows nothing about housing. Plans frequently bus children out of residentially integrated neighborhoods. Perhaps the treatment of integrated neighborhoods is the simplest school-housing issue. Among the districts I visited, only Louisville has an order that explicitly exempts integrated neighborhoods from busing.[13] Denver's 1974 plan exempted a number of neighborhoods, but it has not been updated since.[14] In Charlotte, North Carolina, and Columbus, Ohio, children are bused from most integrated neighborhoods.[15] At its worst, busing is determined by the race of the individual child. In such instances, children who have been enjoying a naturally integrated school in a naturally integrated community may be separated and bused in two directions. This action amounts to punishment of those who actually believe in and practice integrated living.

With little change, integrated neighborhood schools could be exempted from busing. The change would be easier to make if integrated areas were defined as those that had shown some stability. There are few such areas. A 1978 study of the hundreds of schools in Los Angeles, for example, found not one stably integrated black-white school and only a handful of stable Chicano-Anglo schools.[16] The St. Louis school desegregation plan, adopted in May 1980, determined that only two schools in the city could be plausibly exempted. (The judge ordered the exemption extended to an additional school for a one-year trial period.)[17]

Louisville's approach to exemptions, which has been extensively published by the Kentucky Human Rights Commission, could become a model. The Louisville exemption operates in three ways. First, neighborhoods that meet the statistical goals established in the court order are left out of the desegregation plan. Those who move to these areas can be certain that, as long as the neighborhood is integrated, their children will not be bused. Second, to meet the goals established by the desegregation plan, Louisville assigns children to schools individually by race. Thus, when a black family moves into a neighborhood where whites dominate the residential pattern, or vice versa, the family automatically increases integration at the local school and is exempted from busing. Third, new neighborhoods that become well integrated are exempt from busing.

When the Jefferson County (metropolitan Louisville) School Board redrew its boundaries in 1980, several new schools, including one in a distant suburban area, were exempted from busing. Many black families had moved to white suburbs thanks to a special effort by the Kentucky Human Rights Commission to counsel black families about housing opportunities. A counselor drove families around white neighborhoods to help them find housing. About half of the eligible black families chose to live in white areas; about a fourth of these families went to the suburbs.[18] Each move automatically exempted the family from busing. The *Louisville Times* observed, on May 28, 1980:

> The relocation of 722 black families in formerly white neighborhoods has been a silent, but significant change. . . . An important

incentive in this migration has been the fact that black children who live in school districts with white majorities are exempt from busing.[19]

The Kentucky Human Rights Commission has recently received a HUD grant to highlight the connection between school and housing issues. Executive Director Galen Martin notes:

We ... will soon be into a media campaign with billboards, bus placards, bumper stickers, etc., echoing the theme, "Welcome New Neighbors—Housing Desegregation Has Reduced Busing."[20]

The keys to the changes in Louisville were a court order that explicitly recognized the need for special treatment of integrated areas, a plan that provides instant exemptions for families moving into opposite-race areas, and determined and imaginative leadership by Galen Martin, who understood the school-housing relationship from the beginning.

The Louisville approach does not, however, do anything about site selection for subsidized housing. In fact, the interviews for this project turned up a large proposal for subsidized family housing under the Section 8 subsidy program unknown to school authorities, that could significantly unbalance an entire cluster in the city's desegregation plan.[21]

Louisville's accomplishment was not due to unusually favorable attitudes toward residential integration. During 1977 black and white couples conducted tests to determine the extent of housing discrimination in the Louisville suburbs. In 65 of the 70 tests conducted, they found evidence of discrimination. It was often sufficiently subtle that the black testers were not aware they were being discriminated against until they compared their experiences with those of their white counterparts.[22] Progress, then, is possible even in resistant areas.

None of the court orders dealt explicitly with the housing issue in any city visited. In Charlotte, N.C., a separate court case on subsidized housing helped produce an agreement by local officials to site public housing in an integrated fashion.[23]

The lack of any policy sometimes produced bizarre twists. In Minneapolis, where the school board had failed to go to court to obtain a supporting housing policy, it went to court against an integrated neighborhood and won. The neighborhood parents appealed to the school board without success, then sued the board to prevent closing of the integrated neighborhood school. The school lawyers won this case and the school board closed the school.[24] School planners elsewhere, using computers to minimize bus trips, devise plans that integrate segregated neighborhoods by transferring children from nearby integrated neighborhoods. No one points out the absurdity of such "efficiency."

Court orders that impose on school authorities a continuing obligation to deal with the results of spreading residential segregation more often create an incentive for those authorities to involve themselves with housing decisions. Policies that are largely independent of residential patterns, or do not require the board to deal with resegregation, produce little, if any, interest in the problem.

Milwaukee, for example, had a school plan almost totally unrelated to residential patterns. Nowhere was there less sensitivity to housing issues. The Milwaukee plan relied very heavily on magnet schools. Whites did not face mandatory reassignment but only a heavily promoted set of choices about special educational programs designed to produce desegregation. Large numbers of black students were persuaded to transfer. The school district judged its success by the ultimate racial composition of the schools (many of which were wholly unrelated to geographic boundaries). Since the state government paid all the costs, there was no incentive to minimize transportation. The idea was to minimize tension and compulsion, particularly for whites, even if it meant running scores of buses to different destinations through a single neighborhood. It mattered little to the school district when a neighborhood changed, and the district did nothing to monitor or influence such changes.[25]

A November 1980 report by Lois Quinn of the Metropolitan Integration Research Center in Milwaukee underlines some of the consequences of this approach. Voluntary transfer plans in Milwaukee, she suggests, appear to undermine the possibility of maintaining integrated neighborhood schools in the city. Operating integrated neighborhood schools would require holding neighborhood whites in the local school. Under a magnet school plan such as Milwaukee's, however, whites in integrated schools are much more likely than those in all-white schools to move out.[26] (The same pattern was observed by the Los Angeles court-appointed monitoring committee in its study of the Los Angeles magnet-school program.)[27] Lois Quinn reports:

> Under Milwaukee's voluntary choice plan . . . schools in neighborhoods in racial transition are allowed to "tip" due to a lack of white volunteers. Some white families residing in these areas seized the opportunity to leave the neighborhood school, often for schools in white neighborhoods. . . . Black children who remained in the

neighborhood (which still may be majority white) are subjected to segregated black schools. Since neighborhood schools are preserved primarily in the segregated white areas, white families living in transitional neighborhoods may be encouraged by the school desegregation plan to relocate into these areas.[28]

Since integrated neighborhoods can become stable only if they continually attract white as well as minority homebuyers, the fact that the neighborhood school is not virtually all black has to be an obstacle in the stabilization drive.

The participation of the suburbs in the Milwaukee desegregation effort is even more limited and has had no effect at all on housing policy. Of the 48,500 minority students in Milwaukee public schools, 916 attend school in one of 12 cooperating suburban districts under a voluntary transfer plan. The districts remain 93 per cent white. There was no organized effort to move city black families receiving Section 8 housing subsidies out to suburban areas where they would need no busing, as in Louisville. City minority families are not allowed to use their subsidy certificates outside city limits, and the county subsidizes all of its assisted black families in housing inside the city. This was particularly unfortunate for the families sending their children out to the suburbs. About half of those families told researchers that they would consider moving to the community where their children were attending school but that the biggest obstacle was money. Nearly 60 per cent said that they would be interested in a move to the suburb if a subsidy were available.[29] There was interest but no mechanism.

The voluntary nature of the Milwaukee plan did not prevent action on housing. It minimized the pressure on white officials, however, and created no incentive for housing analysis or initiatives.

At the other end of the spectrum is Charlotte, where the court required the school board to redistrict any school in the metropolitan area that was becoming more than half black. As soon as the neighborhood changed, the school officials had a new problem. If that change was the result of a decision by housing officials, the school officials had an obvious interest in ensuring that such decisions were not repeated. The fact that the housing authority had been sued and a consent order signed against further violations increased the potential leverage of the school board.

The problem emerged quickly in Charlotte. One school that was substantially integrated on a residential basis was left out of the busing plan as an experiment. Housing officials decided to locate subsidized housing there. The result, given the fact that the greater majority of Charlotte public-housing families are black, was to rapidly resegregate the delicately balanced school. School officials attacked the action and demanded consultation on future decisions.[30] Charlotte school, housing, and planning officials and local selected leaders now have the best-developed system for consultation and coordinated planning of sites for new construction of subsidized housing that I found in any of the cities I studied. (The city, however, lacks counseling of the Louisville kind.)

The mere fact that a school board must cope with the consequences of residential resegregation does not, of course, guarantee that the community will take appropriate action. In Champaign, Ill., for example, there are state board-of-education regulations requiring readjustment of any school whose racial composition deviates more than 15 per cent from the systemwide racial statistics (about 26 per cent black and 3 per cent Asian). The Champaign Housing Authority, however, failed to build the scattered-site housing authorized by HUD between 1973 and 1980, when it lost the authorization. The city recently recommended construction of a substantial new, subsidized subdivision for blacks in the ghetto. The school board has said nothing about this issue. Nor did it comment on a proposal for subsidized suburban housing that could have helped desegregation but faced harsh neighborhood criticism.

In Champaign, as in many other communities, the various governmental authorities reported that they had never discussed the issue, even though the school district faced a major controversy over the boundary adjustments required by desegregation. The city council's policy was that the schools were a separate taxing unit and should run separately. The planning department did no planning based on the school data. Communication between the city and the independent housing authority was limited. The regional planning commission did not consult the schools about housing proposals.

Major Joan Severns pointed out that the housing authority and the city had little enthusiasm for low-income housing, and the city had little authority to do anything in the field.[31] Champaign illustrates why it may be almost as difficult to coordinate policy in a municipality with a relative handful of government employees as it is in Washington. After thirteen years of successful busing, the school authorities could not expect any help from other municipal officials. Local housing officials showed neither understanding nor leadership. The school board had to adopt a new plan in 1981 to deal with demographic changes in the city.

CAN THE COURTS ORDER A COORDINATED POLICY?

As litigators came to understand the relationship between school and housing desegregation policies, they made efforts during 1980 to devise interlocking policies. The Department of Justice responded to criticism of its uncoordinated enforcement strategy by launching simultaneous investigations of school and housing violations in several cities and sharing investigatory responsibility with the Department of Education. A consent agreement was negotiated by the Justice Department in Chicago, and one important court order highlighted the possibility of a major change in the perspective of federal agencies on the question. If the federal courts and executive agencies will require or strongly encourage coordinated action, the likelihood that the issue will receive serious attention at the local level will increase.

The May 21, 1980, St. Louis court order embodied the most fully developed approach so far to the school-housing relationship, and it set off the most massive planning effort to develop a coordinated approach.[32] The city's school desegregation plan, approved in the court order, contains a number of housing-related features. It exempts integrated neighborhoods from busing and guarantees any neighborhood that becomes integrated in the future a neighborhood school as long as it remains integrated. The plan provides integrated schools for the reviving neighborhoods that were attracting whites but still had all-black neighborhood schools. Any integrated neighborhood that becomes virtually all black or any reviving neighborhood that becomes virtually all white will have to resume busing. An incentive is thus created for an integration-stabilization policy in both kinds of areas.

Any white neighborhood that accepts sufficient subsidized housing to produce a 20 per cent black public school enrollment will get back its neighborhood school. (Other children can still be bused in if necessary.) The city school enrollment is more than three-fourths black, but the emphasis of the school plan is not on making every school reflect this ratio (as in Cleveland). Rather, it is on achieving as much stability as possible in substantially integrated schools with approximately equal numbers of blacks and whites. The school district will have to make annual readjustments to deal with schools that fall substantially outside this range.[33]

The novel feature of the St. Louis order, however, is the directive that the city government, the school board, the state government, and the federal departments of HUD and Justice devise a plan to administer the federal housing programs in the St. Louis metropolitan area in a way that will support integrated schools.

Following this order HUD Secretary Moon Landrieu appointed a task force within HUD to develop a federal response. In St. Louis, the staff of the city's Community Development Agency convened a group of housing experts, planners, local HUD officials, suburban agency staff, academic experts, and others to work out a local response. Both plans were submitted to the federal court in late November 1980.[34] They deal with a wide range of programs that could have a positive impact on residential integration and will guarantee far better communication and consultation over the issue in the future. The same issue is likely to be raised in other school desegregation cases.

Litigation can forcefully call the issue to the attention of local officials. But issues are complex and require many decisions over many years to achieve a substantial positive effect. The courts are unlikely to produce a final resolution.

Sorting Out Strategies

Desegregation is often described simply as the process of opening up opportunities in white areas and white institutions to blacks and Hispanics, but this is actually only one of several processes involved. To develop a strategy for coordinated school and housing desegregation, planners must understand and explicitly state each of these processes.

Interviews for this report and analysis of other research reveal three fundamental policy goals:

1) achieving stable integration in areas that now have both white and minority residents

2) opening up segregated white neighborhoods, schools, and job sites to blacks and Hispanics

3) preserving substantial integration in inner-city neighborhoods, where revitalization pressures are so strong that a minority community may be transformed into another Georgetown, with residence limited to wealthy whites and a handful of wealthy minority families

Although most public discussion focuses on breaching the wall of segregation in all-white areas, some of the easiest and most significant gains could be made in desegregated communities and schools threatened by resegregation. Substantial numbers of people live in such communities in every major metropolitan area. Neither the whites nor the minority families who live there want resegregation and ghettoization. Often these communities provide homes for whites who cannot afford to move and for upwardly mobile black and Hispanic families seeking better opportunities for their children than they have found in the ghetto or the barrio. Their common interest in stability could form the basis for a powerful political constituency supporting integrationist policies. In some communities it already does.

Since communities are continually changing, the problem of maintaining well-integrated neighborhoods with integrated schools is essentially one of creating an equilibrium among streams of black, white, and Hispanic homeseekers who are continually moving, and being channeled, to specific parts of metropolitan areas. Achieving integrated schools through housing policies requires that integration be substantial, that it be integration of families with school-age children, and that it be maintained. Most contemporary residential integration, unfortunately, falls into one or more of the following categories:

- substantial but temporary (communities bordering existing ghettos or barrios)
- substantial but for adults only (urban-renovation or condominium areas with rental housing)
- stable but token (upper-income areas)
- substantial but limited to housing (whites almost totally dependent on private schools)

The research literature shows that substantially integrated neighborhoods and schools tend to rapidly resegregate. Most major U.S. cities have no census tracts that have ever been stably integrated.[35] Most have few, if any, stably integrated neighborhood elementary schools.

The problem is not that we have not had integrated neighborhoods or schools; we have had great numbers. The problem is that we couldn't keep them and that we usually did not try. In fact, the courts often find evidence of actions by school boards or housing authorities that have speeded up the process of undermining integrated communities. Left alone, the market almost invariably resegregates such communities by steering in minority homeseekers and steering white homeseekers elsewhere. Thus, any housing subsidy policy that simply pumps money into the market is very likely to accelerate resegregation. Any school policy that permits white students to transfer out (for example, optional attendance zones) or rigidly holds to a neighborhood assignment policy is likely to speed resegregation. Only organized and conscious action can defeat the process.

To achieve stability there must be a continuing balance in the real estate market. Since the average family moves every six years, communities actually replace a significant portion of their population each year. To integrate the schools, both white and black families with school-age children, must be continually moving into the community.

ATTACK ON RACIAL TRANSITION

To maintain integration, it is necessary to attack racial transition at several levels. (Each of these is discussed in the pages that follow.)

- by testing and punishing steering by realtors
- by strong community action against overt discrimination and panic peddling
- by action against redlining of integrated communities by mortgage finance institutions or insurance companies or both
- by code enforcement to maintain quality of housing and avoid conversion for alternative uses, and by strategic investment of city or federal funds to prevent the first signs of deterioration
- by instructing realtors on community-school relationships, to avoid stereotypes about "changing" neighborhoods
- by developing centers for housing counseling
- by school public relations and recruitment efforts
- by developing integrated magnet schools or special programs in local schools (it is easiest to draw both minority and white students to an integrated site)
- by involving neighborhood organizations, such as churches, in school and housing efforts
- by introducing human relations training in the schools
- by careful administration, site selection, and counseling on Section 8 existing, Section 8 new construction, and public housing programs to avoid use of public financing to turn integrated communities into ghettos
- by exempting the neighborhood school from busing out school children as long as it remains substantially integrated
- by preferential treatment of integrated neighborhood schools in school-closing decisions (closing these creates the most substantial cost increases, because busing may well go from zero to 100 per cent)
- by obtaining guarantees from the school district that substantial school integration will be maintained even if it is necessary to bus in students from outside
- by commitment to scattered-site subsidized housing for families, to maintain integration if community rapidly gentrifies
- by strong police presence and convincing attention to security problems

Testing Steering by Realtors. To stabilize communities and their schools it is necessary to brake the momentum of resegregation. This momentum rests on the discriminatory actions of powerful forces in the housing market and on the knowledge, expectations, and prejudices of families searching for housing and schools. Realtors and lending institutions expect such communities to become all-minority and to decline. Many of them associate racial change with deterioration of property, increase in violence, decline of educational quality, and other negatives. Usually they consider it appropriate to recommend property purchase by minority families looking for better homes and schools. They consider it unfair, however, to recommend property purchase to whites, who would find themselves committed to a declining nonwhite community.[36] The expectation is that the school will rapidly resegregate and become inferior. These are extremely powerful prophecies in the hands of people who possess the ability to make them come true. In most communities they are rapidly fulfilled.

Part of the steering process concerns the schools. A recent study of real estate ads in 14 metropolitan areas revealed that, with few exceptions, the schools and school districts named in the ads were almost all white.[37] A study of real estate marketing practices by testers in Seattle indicated powerful steering of white families away from the city. The realtors conveyed negative information about the entire city school system, which has been a national leader in locally designed desegregation without a court order. When white couples told realtors that they were interested in living in an integrated city neighborhood, the realtors often replied that the schools were bad and that they should look in the suburbs.[38]

Fair-housing enforcement seldom addresses the complex process of ghetto creation. Enforcement is very small-scale, often fails to resolve even the few cases investigated, seldom effectively attacks systemic problems, and is wholly inadequate on subtle problems such as steering.

During the first eight years of the federal fair-housing law, the Department of Justice completed enforcement of approximately 23 cases per year for the entire nation. There were 18 states in which no Justice Department case was resolved during the first eight years.[39] Even in the New York Metropolitan area, home of the nation's largest national civil rights groups and center of the earliest fair-housing efforts, enforcement activities in the late 1970s were minuscule. According to the Regional Plan Association, HUD successfully resolved only about one complaint in 20 that it received.[40] HUD's recent national fair-housing study showed that extensive discrimination was commonplace.[41] HUD has no enforcement power, merely the right to investigate and conciliate. In 1980, Congress debated legislation to give HUD enforcement authority, but it was killed in the Senate after the GOP election victory.[42]

Field research based on testing of realtors shows that much discrimination has taken on such subtle forms that it is difficult or impossible for a black or Hispanic family to identify unfair treatment. The realtor shows them houses, including houses in integrated neighborhoods, and appears friendly. Only when similar white testers go to the same realtor and are shown different houses, offered more assistance, and steered away from the integrated neighborhood blacks or Hispanics were shown does it become possible to discern a pattern of discrimination. What is represented to minority families as a well-integrated, desirable area to live in is being described, at the same time, to whites as a rapidly changing area that would not be a good investment for them. Sometimes they are told the schools are poor or "changing." Treatment that seems legal and fair on the surface can rapidly create ghettos and undermine hope for stability in integrated neighborhoods. It can only be countered by systemic enforcement with testers. In the fair-housing enforcement process, no serious attention has been paid to the role of schools in neighborhood resegregation.

Although steering is a key problem, it is seldom prosecuted. Civil rights offices usually concentrate on processing individual complaints filed by persons facing overt discrimination. These are certainly the clearest, simplest, and least ambiguous cases, but they seldom have any impact beyond the housing unit affected. In fact, the process is often so slow that the complainant has been forced to buy or rent elsewhere. So few of these cases are pursued that the risk of prosecution can be safely discounted.

Community Action. Racial steering and associated problems of integrated areas—panic peddling, blockbusting, and redlining—are attacked principally by residents of older central-city or inner suburban neighborhoods faced with decline or racial transition or both. Only well-organized communities seem capable of putting up a real fight—elsewhere people just leave. The most fully developed campaigns—including extensive testing, publicity, ordinances prohibiting the display of For Sale signs on lawns, community-group demonstrations against realtors, and litigation—have been undertaken by neighborhood associations or suburban governments that have mobilized communities against the threat of ghetto creation. In some Chicago and Cleveland suburbs, for example, there has been extensive activity on this issue, including special training programs for realtors, efforts to create real estate counseling institutions, and even attempts to require special local licensing of realtors before they can work in a community.[43]

Combating Redlining. The assertion that mortgage finance institutions and insurance companies reject applications from black, Hispanic, integrated, or poor white communities—the redlining issue—has been the subject of numerous reports and community demands for reform and some legislative activity. Much less controversial than overtly racial questions, redlining has stimulated federal, state, and local efforts to report and regulate it and to offer incentives for more equitable treatment.[44] The problem is by no means solved; it remains a component of the ghetto-creation process in some areas.

Preventing Decay. Those struggling to stabilize integrated areas have to deal convincingly with widely held stereotypes. Many leaders of neighborhood organizations believe, for example, that neighborhoods undergoing racial change receive a declining quality of public service, including less rigorous building-code enforcement. The leaders argue that local officials tend to write off integrated areas as future ghettos and slums, and by cutting services help fulfill their own prophecies.

These fears can be fought by intensified code enforcement and rapid action against blight in integrated areas. A number of integrated suburbs, including University City, Ohio, have rigid inspection and occupancy-permit ordinances that forbid transfer of property without correction of violations. The suburbs also tend to use community development funds to take strong action against the first signs of blight in integrated areas. A new study shows that families in integrated areas are highly sensitive to signs of physical decay.[45] Cities seldom have such policies for integrated areas.

One of the simplest policy issues concerns physical deterioration. According to the self-fulfilling prophecy of neighborhood transition, once racial change begins the quality of housing decays. This means, of course, that any sign of decay can be extremely destructive, because it is interpreted as tangible evidence of ghetto development. A recent study of integrated communities in Chicago revealed a high level of sensitivity to the physical character of the neighborhood.[46]

Communities working for stability usually pay strict attention to preventing deterioration by rigid inspection, targeted public improvements, and property-transfer controls. Central cities, however, have many competing priorities. Decay, of course, can be attacked most cheaply and effectively in its early stages. But in the cities, the need to stabilize changing areas must compete with the needs of much more deteriorated areas that have problems of enormous magnitude. Given the shrinking real resources of many cities, federal community development funds are among the few available sources of discretionary grants.

Because this money is often restricted to severely deteriorated "target" areas, its more efficient use may be blocked. To rehabilitate one severely deteriorated housing unit in the heart of a ghetto might cost $30,000. Yet the same money could prevent minor deterioration of 10 houses in an area just beginning to integrate, thus affecting perceptions about the future for private investment. Strategies to stabilize changing communities should be an important part of community development plans. Federal guidelines should encourage early attention to these issues.

Training Realtors. Since realtors play a key role in ghetto creation and their views of school quality are important, it is only common sense that communities facing negative steering should attempt to instruct realtors and provide them with better information. In Oak Park, Ill., for example, there is a very close relationship between the community and the local realtors. The community, just across the street from a part of Chicago's West Side ghetto, has worked continually with the realtors. The Oak Park Board of Realtors now supports efforts to maintain an integrated housing market, unlike the National Association of Realtors, headquartered a few miles away in the Chicago Loop.[47] When tested, Oak Park realtors made favorable comments about the local schools.[48]

Housing Counseling. Without strong outside intervention, the housing market resegregates the great majority of integrated communities. Housing subsidy programs that work through the private market almost always place low-income minority families in segregated or racially transitional communities.[49] Unless special efforts are made to counteract the forces of racial resegregation, the vigorous enforcement of fair-housing laws and granting of market-oriented rent subsidies to large numbers of black and Hispanic families is likely to speed up the processes of ghetto and barrio expansion.

Neighborhood organizations and housing developers have been attempting to intervene to forestall racial change since the 1920s. Until recently, however, the efforts were usually almost wholly negative—designed to produce stability by excluding minorities. Integration requires very different and positive efforts.

The perception that integration is merely the brief time between the entrance of the first black into an area and the departure of the last white is a persistent stereotype. There is a general belief—among realtors, among families in neighborhoods near ghettos, and among members of the community at large—that any significant integration of a community near a black settlement results in its rapid incorporation in an expanding ghetto. Indeed, few communities have had stable residential integration and even fewer have stable neighborhood school integration. Karl and Alma Taeuber's classic study, *Negroes in Cities*, found a consistent pattern of racial transition in major cities.[50] A study of movement patterns in integrated neighborhoods across the U.S. showed that about four-fifths of the neighborhoods were in transition. The stable ones usually had rental housing intended for adults only; thus families with children, those most likely to stabilize integrated schools, were being excluded.[51] A 1980 study of integrated Chicago neighborhoods found that few whites with children in public schools were moving in.[52]

To remain integrated, a neighborhood must continually attract both black and white families. The great majority of American families are homeowners, and most neighborhoods are dominated by single-family homes. The typical American moves every six years, and there is continual movement in and out of every community. To stabilize integration, communities must continually attract white as well as minority families that will buy houses.

An attempt to intervene directly in the housing market, counseling sets up informal real estate marketing procedures. In recent years, some counseling groups have become interracial, with the explicit goal of organizing both blacks and whites in a community to try to preserve integration. There is even a national organization, the Exchange Congress, of communities working to preserve integration.[53]

The most fully developed efforts have produced housing offices whose basic task is to counter steering by realtors, and self-steering by individual homeseekers. These housing offices, with the full cooperation of some elements in the local community, actively seek to promote a positive community image and keep whites as well as minority families in the local housing market. There is usually a large and active market among blacks for housing in good-quality integrated neighborhoods. Until stability is achieved, therefore, much effort must be devoted to attracting new white families while encouraging blacks to seek housing in all-white neighborhoods or in surrounding white communities.

Housing offices report that schools are a crucial consideration in recruiting white families. Officials in Teaneck, N.J., Shaker Heights, Ohio, Park Forest, Ill., and other integrated communities report that the schools' reputation is extremely important in maintaining integration in the city. The equally important correlative is that the schools can only remain integrated if the housing does. This is recognized by school authorities, who usually cooperate with housing efforts by introducing prospective residents to individual schools. In Teaneck, one of the first integrated New York suburbs to have integrated schools, each school welcomes visitors and provides information for those considering a move to the community.[54] A more direct connection has been developed in Shaker Heights, where the local school board paid one-third of the cost of the community's housing office from the time of its foundation.[55]

Through counseling, these housing offices are in a position to deal directly with public stereotypes and to promote the community. They are also in a key position to reward realtors and rental agents who support integration efforts and to punish those who oppose them. Properly administered, housing offices make a critical difference in influencing the course of integration, especially if their efforts are closely coordinated with related community activities.

Another kind of counseling is critical both to stabilizing integrated areas and to increasing integration in white areas (these will be discussed in the next chapter). This is counseling for families receiving rent subsidies. These are usually minority families with young children, and they usually remain where they are or move nearby. If they move in large numbers into integrated areas, they spur resegregation of a neighborhood and its school. Indeed, this problem is at the root of the most notable case of school resegregation in the operation of the metropolitan Wilmington desegregation plan.[56] A concerted effort to open up more choices for minority families receiving the subsidies, to acquaint them with unfamiliar neighborhoods, and to avoid steering and self-steering based on limited information can have a powerful impact. Doing nothing imperils integrated areas.

Stabilizing integrated communities probably requires a major effort, at the same time, to open up segregated white communities. Unless stabilization efforts include a strong commitment to opening up more opportunities for minority families, they could be legitimately criticized for restricting minority housing choices.

School Public Relations. Schools desiring to remain integrated without constant readjustments to their desegregation plans must realize that they are competing for white families with powerful interests marketing a strongly positive image of settlement in new, all-white suburbs, away from the problems of the city. This is where most new family housing is built, and there is a large investment in creating favorable images to sell houses. School public relations must also recognize and frankly confront the negative public image of integrated public schools.

A basic assumption of school desegregation litigation is that minority schools should be integrated because they are "inherently unequal"—not because there is anything wrong with minority children, but because there is something fundamentally wrong about the stereotyped views of minority institutions in a society controlled by whites. White society expects minority institutions to be inferior and acts in ways that fulfill that expectation.

The strength of the prejudice is evident in this: Thousands of school districts have experimented with open enrollment patterns, yet rarely has even one white child transferred to a black or Hispanic school. When special magnet programs, offering superior educational opportunities, are located in minority neighborhoods of big cities, they rarely receive significant numbers of transfers. A survey in San Diego, for instance, showed that most whites would not transfer their children to a school that was demonstrably superior.[57]

Researchers asked Seattle families that moved to the suburbs between 1974 and 1976 about their reasons for moving. The most common reason, cited by 37 per cent of those questioned, was "dissatisfaction with the schools in the city."[58] A 1977 study for the Berkeley, Calif., school district found that stereotypes about the Berkeley schools were widespread, in spite of a strong academic record. Interviews disclosed "four times as many negative feelings than [sic] positive sentiments."[59]

> Negative general comments used more colorful phrases such as "lousy," "rowdy," "chaotic," "anarchic," "messy," "ugly," "ineffective" or "non-productive." The essence of this stereotype is that the Berkeley system is "not doing its job," that other districts are better. . . .[60]

The study group recommended to the school district that it launch an aggressive effort to publicize the positive attributes of the schools. Specifically, it proposed that Berkeley "institutionalize a districtwide public relations and orientation program directed at potential new and incoming parents."[61]

In contrast to some suburban school systems, the integrated large-city systems I visited for this report had made no significant effort to work with realtors or provide them with good public-relations materials on their schools. Nor had they worked with the national transfer services or large employers—groups that often play a key role in determining where families moving from city to city search for houses.

Large-city school districts are usually complex, self-contained bureaucracies with little experience in outreach and little skill in public relations. They are unaccustomed to thinking of these activities as a permanent necessity. They viewed as temporary the large-scale public-relations efforts that launched desegregation.

Several cities have got beyond thinking about the public-relations problem; they are attempting to recruit students who would otherwise stay away because of the stereotypes. The metropolitan Nashville, Tenn., district tried to cope with public attitudes about desegregation by making an aggressive effort to publicize their schools' positive qualities. The technique used, according to schools' information director, was "an information flood." During the 1977 convention of the National School Public Relations Association, the Jackson, Miss., schools reported a sharp increase in white enrollment. Richmond, Va., officials recruited at shopping centers and advertised on radio and television; those in Norfolk, Va., reported working with realtors.[62] These are exceptions. Integrated school systems in segregated metropolitan areas must learn to counter stereotypes if they are to remain integrated. This is a high-priority need.

Magnet-School Programs. One way to stabilize integrated neighborhoods may be to offer, at integrated sites, uniquely attractive school programs that will draw students from beyond the neighborhood. The neighborhood public elementary school usually changes its racial composition faster than does the neighborhood. If the school is to remain integrated its composition must not be limited by the demographic trends in the immediate area. Minority families arriving in integrated communities usually have more and younger children than do their white neighbors. Also, they are far more likely to send their children to public schools. Thus, the minority enrollment percentage in the neighborhood primary school is often two to three times the overall minority enrollment percentage in the neighborhood.[63] A school that becomes overwhelmingly non-white undermines its chances of attracting white families.

Probably the best way to break the link between schools and housing in neighborhood transition is to adopt a school desegregation plan that makes all schools in the metropolitan area approximately similar in racial composition and ends the connection between neighborhood and school resegregation.[64] In the absence of such plans, however, some of the same goals can be achieved in certain circumstances by offering special educational programs drawing volunteer students from a broad area into an integrated neighborhood.

A national study of magnet schools found that they were a poor tool for desegregating large school systems, since they usually failed to draw white transfers into schools in minority neighborhoods.[65] They can work, however, as a set of educational choices within a mandatory plan if whites know they are going to be moved anyway. An extensive study of the magnet schools in Los Angeles' desegregation plan in the school year 1978–79 indicated that *only* those located in integrated neighborhoods drew well from both Anglo and minority communities. Magnet schools in segregated neighborhoods usually remained largely Anglo, Hispanic, or black.[66] An integrated community may be an ideal site for magnet programs, one in which both white and minority children feel less threatened and more welcome. In the case of small suburbs, this approach might require drawing volunteer transfer students from across school-district boundary lines. In two states, this type of transfer can be subsidized under state law with aid from federal school desegregation funds.[67]

Explicit policies to encourage and finance such transfers are needed in the states that do not have them. State policies and federal court orders that emphasize desegregation within single districts are not appropriate in rapidly changing suburban communities. They should be reviewed and replaced by policies strongly encouraging solutions that involve students from a broader geographic area. Small suburbs change racial composition as fast as does a city neighborhood. In Illinois, for example, all of the districts undergoing the most rapid racial change are in the Chicago suburbs, near growing ghettos.[68] The federal government should consider developing explicit policies in the Emergency School Aid Act (ESAA) magnet-school program, giving preference to schools located in integrated areas.

At a recent meeting in Cleveland, the mayor of a successfully integrated suburb said that the central problem the community faced was the difficulty of attracting sufficient white children to keep its schools integrated.[69] Bellwood, a community in the

Chicago suburbs that went to the Supreme Court to defend its aggressive efforts for housing stabilization and won, is troubled by rapid school resegregation. A state policy requires racial-balance busing within the district, whose white enrollment is plummeting, but does nothing to involve adjacent white communities.[70] Regional suburban magnet schools could be part of the answer.

Involving Neighborhood Organizations. To stabilize integration, it is usually necessary to mobilize local organizations to work toward this goal. Book-length case studies of Oak Park, Ill., Teaneck, N.J., and the Hyde Park community in Chicago, as well as numerous shorter reports on other city and suburban communities, suggest that community organization is essential to prevent panic, to monitor real estate practices, to work for successful integration, and to keep the integrated community attractive to both white and minority home buyers.[71] Permanent efforts may be unnecessary.

Creating the expectation that the community will remain integrated is difficult. In some special circumstances, major community efforts to maintain integration may not be required. For example, integration may survive where housing costs are very high, because the number of potential minority home buyers is limited. Also, in communities marked by widespread gentrification and huge speculative gains in property values, market forces may maintain and expand white housing demand even though the schools remain all black. (In fact, there may be a danger of resegregation by pushing out poor minority families.) Ordinarily, however, involvement of community organizations is essential to maintain integration.

Public policies should recognize the importance of community organizations in maintaining integration. Holding and attracting students to an integrated school, for example, requires more community outreach than operating a school in an ordinary segregated neighborhood. Fears and stereotypes of white parents can best be addressed through personal contact. Cooperative planning of schools and housing with neighborhood organizations and small grants to strengthen their operations could be important parts of stabilization efforts.

Human-Relations Training Within School Systems. An important factor in maintaining integrated neighborhoods with integrated schools is good race relations in the schools. People who live in or move into integrated neighborhoods usually support integrated schools, but do not wish their children to face racial tensions. Blacks, Hispanics, and whites who live in such communities comment that segregation often develops within schools, especially at upper grade levels. Small conflicts can stir fears and rumors.

After a court order there is often a crash effort in human relations for a few months, but then the effort is dropped. If school districts wish to encourage stable integration, race-relations issues must be followed up. Research has identified some keys to successful race relations at the school level.[72] They are:

- selecting principals who support integration and are viewed by teachers as strong educational leaders
- desegregating the faculty
- developing disciplinary rules that each racial group sees as fair
- avoiding tracking (rigid separation of children, classified according to ability, with different curricula), particularly in the elementary grades
- seating students interracially in classrooms and including in the curriculum some academic projects that require cooperative efforts by interracial groups

Explicit efforts to improve race relations in the school can be very beneficial. School officers, particularly the principal, must be accessible and fair to each group of parents, if community confidence is to be maintained. Many people leave their neighborhoods because of school problems that could have been avoided. In integrated neighborhoods, work on these issues is an important continuing responsibility.

Avoiding Government-Financed Resegregation. Administrators of housing subsidy programs should handle with special sensitivity neighborhoods that have substantially integrated schools. If a public housing project is built there, or new Section 8 construction located there, it should be with a strong program of tenant assignment that explicitly supports integration. Because of the great importance of the neighborhood's appearance, it should be as compatible as possible with the community, avoiding evidence of community decline. A neighborhood with only minority children will almost surely upset the equilibrium of the elementary school, which has a capacity of about 300 students. (That number is small enough to be substantially affected by a small number of families.) If a city lacks white applicants on its waiting list for subsidized housing, or lacks the commitment to counseling and tenant recruitment necessary to produce integration, it should not build subsidized housing projects in delicately balanced neighborhoods because they will spur transition. Few cities have the sophistication necessary to manage these tasks successfully.

Proper administration of the Section 8 program, which subsidizes individual families in individual private-market housing units, could help rather than hurt integrated neighborhoods. This program needs a strong counseling effort so that minority families are not simply funneled into already integrated areas, resegregating them with the rent subsidy program.

Exempting Schools from Busing. All participants in school desegregation litigation—school boards, civil rights groups, city officials, neighborhood leaders, and the courts themselves—share a common interest in avoiding busing that is counterproductive to the long-term goal of an integrated society with naturally integrated schools. Plans should exempt schools in well-integrated, stable neighborhoods from busing of their children, and should offer the incentive of exemption to additional neighborhoods that become residentially integrated in the future, as in the St. Louis plan.

Keeping Integrated Schools Open. Perhaps the most controversial decision school districts face today, apart from desegregation itself, is the closing of excess schools. Districts with rapidly falling enrollments are finding themselves with as many as twice the number of schools they need. There are high fixed costs for providing energy, maintenance, and administrators in excess buildings. As fiscal pressures grow, school boards must make difficult choices between closing schools or cutting programs and firing teachers. Half-empty junior and senior high schools lack enough students to offer a proper range of elective courses. Every community, however, fights strenuously to keep its school.

In racial terms, the decisions are just as important as the site and boundary decisions of earlier decades, which the courts have so often found to be an important cause of segregated education. Closing decisions involve choices between neighborhoods and precipitate large-scale redrawing of school attendance boundaries. The new lines should increase integration.

Schools in integrated neighborhoods should not be closed unless they are in exceptionally poor condition. In a city with a desegregation plan, closing a walk-in integrated school means that all of its students will probably be bused, whereas none was bused before. This action creates the highest possible percentage increase in the costs of desegregation. Integrated areas should be rewarded by having their integrated schools kept intact although other schools are closed.

Guaranteeing Future School Integration. If a central problem of maintaining integration is the fear that it won't last, perhaps the most effective solution would be a solid school-district guarantee that integration would be maintained. A strong, clear pledge to bring in students as required to maintain integration might give families that need public schools much more confidence in remaining in integrated areas or buying there.

This guarantee is provided, indirectly, in communities with metropolitan desegregation plans and in those with stable districtwide desegregation plans. In metropolitan plans, the family is told that their school will be like all other schools regardless of any demographic change in the neighborhood. In stable districtwide plans, which are often found in cities or suburbs with relatively small minority populations, a family can have a good deal of confidence about the future. Such a guarantee, however, is almost never available where confidence is lowest—in the neighborhoods of large cities or inner suburbs that are right next to a rapidly expanding ghetto or barrio. In two such areas, on the southwest side of Chicago, guarantees were offered by the Chicago school board.[73]

The guarantee was provided for two high schools—Gage Park and Morgan Park—near communities that had undergone rapid and bitter racial change. In the community of Morgan Park, Martin Luther King's fair-housing marches of the 1950s had faced violent resistance. The guarantee operated primarily by limiting the number of black students who could enter the schools. Those who could not be accommodated were offered transfers to other integrated schools. The program did not end the decline of white enrollment, some of which was inevitable with or without desegregation. But it did prevent rapid racial change in the school; it maintained a substantial level of integration for those in attendance; and it offered a rare example of relatively stable school integration in southwest Chicago.[74] Because the mechanism chosen put virtually all of the burden on blacks, however, the plan was challenged by the National Association for the Advancement of Colored People. The Chicago school board dropped it in late 1980.[75]

The Chicago plan is obviously not the only way the goal could be pursued. In the Chicago schools, for example, integration could have been retained by busing in white students from areas that were still all white rather than busing out black students to other integrated schools. If the guarantee of continued integration in the local school is a key element of stability, and the problem cannot be addressed by a broad desegregation plan, the issue of neighborhood-level guarantees must be examined.

Renovation and Integration

Since the beginning of the modern ghetto system, racial change, in most urban neighborhoods, has only increased minority populations. The exceptions have been areas where urban-renewal programs destroyed poor black communities and built new white or integrated housing for middle- and upper-class families.

Until recently the few examples—such as Georgetown in Washington, D.C., and Society Hill in Philadelphia—of neighborhood revitalization in old communities were considered unique and of little broad consequence. In the last few years, however, the process of white immigration to selected neighborhoods has escalated rapidly in some cities, creating a major new racial issue. During the 1950s and 1960s urban renewal was denounced as "Negro removal." Now skyrocketing speculation in numerous neighborhoods in San Francisco, Washington, St. Louis, Chicago, Boston, and other cities is seen as a white plot to push minority families out of locations made more desirable by the energy crisis. A number of black leaders have expressed very serious concern.[76]

The evidence to date shows that there is still a large net loss of whites and middle-income families in older central cities. It is certain, however, that black and Hispanic renters, and poor renters in general, have been pushed out of some hot urban neighborhoods—from Capitol Hill in Washington to the Wilshire Corridor in Los Angeles. In Washington, where the trend is most fully developed, there has been a small increase in the white percentage of the city's population (though it remains about three-fourths black).[77]

It is feared that after a long cycle of renovation and speculation, a depressed black or Hispanic community could end up as an extremely expensive, highly fashionable, and virtually all-white community. This is happening today in some neighborhoods.

The process of racial change in a largely white community brings with it a risk of resegregation and a possible opportunity for stable integration. Similarly, a transition in the opposite direction brings risk but also some important opportunities that have seldom been systematically explored. It is important to devise policies that will increase integration and respond to minority fears of displacement.

At least one important advantage is offered by revitalization—few of the whites who move into reviving neighborhoods in the early phases fear racial integration; many prefer integrated communities. Whites with highly developed racial stereotypes would hardly choose to live in predominantly black areas. But when change becomes very rapid, the high prices of old brownstones, to which few upper-income blacks are attracted, usually lead to re-segregation, in the absence of policies designed to keep the community integrated.

From an integrationist standpoint, this can be the worst of all worlds: The opportunity for residential integration is lost and school integration is not achieved, even in the transitional period during which the community has minority and white residents in large numbers. The revitalization process often begins with neighborhood schools that are completely black or Hispanic. Few white families with young children move in and send children to public schools. Usually, the returning whites are young couples without children, older couples, young professional singles, gays, and a small number of families with children in private schools. If there is to be stable integration in communities that are becoming gentrified, residential integration must be retained and public school integration must be initiated.

RESIDENTIAL POLICIES
Any number of policies could be employed to retain integration. City housing administrators sensitive to the direction of revitalization and real estate speculation could use housing and community development funds to purchase land or buildings, or both, while they are still on the periphery of change (and still available at modest costs), for subsidized housing. Local ordinances can help. For example, landlords in the rental market often discriminate against children, and since minority families are far more likely than whites to be renters, an ordinance forbidding discrimination against children might have a positive impact.[78] Similarly, there are approaches that could limit the negative impact of either condominium conversion of existing rental housing or the construction of new complexes of expensive housing in areas being upgraded.

In some communities, for example, condominium conversion ordinances require, as a condition for obtaining conversion permits, setting aside a certain fraction of the units for low-cost rental by prior tenants. In other areas there is a strong effort to build new mixed-use buildings, combining market-rate housing with subsidized units. The city Community Development Agency in St. Louis, for example, is encouraging extensive construction with 80 per cent market-rate and 20 per cent subsidized units.[79] Such construction may help maintain integration in neighborhoods being renovated if blacks are threatened with displacement. Efforts could be made to attract black professionals, who usually live in the suburbs, by explaining to them the advantages of investment in the city and by showing them examples of beautifully restored row houses. Blacks often see less charm in the idea of moving back (and know less about its financial advantages) than do young white professionals who grew up in suburbs, where they were bored.

In most renovated areas, some minority families own homes or small rental properties. A major strategy for keeping these communities integrated should include special inducements to low-income families to stay in the neighborhood. Small loans or grants for repairing code violations or for cosmetic rehabilitation would be useful to the families and the neighborhoods. Special tax treatment is an urgent necessity, because property values climb much faster than the families' incomes. Legal advice could be helpful in preventing loss of property and avoiding prohibitive taxation between generations.

Where gentrification is under way, a specific strategy is required to ensure that minority residents share in the upward momentum of the neighborhood and the financial gains that come with it. When public funds support renovation, strict planning can prevent their use to drive poor minority families into ghettos or racially changing neighborhoods elsewhere.

The renovation process can offer great rewards to cities if its negative racial consequences can be avoided. At a time when cities and federal agencies have little money for major public projects, renovation improves available housing and greatly increases taxable property values at a minimal cost to government. At a time when middle-class families, with their wealth, skills, and experience, have abandoned cities in very large numbers, the renovation process can bring some of them back—and, in addition, provide important leadership for the city. The process can even improve the psychological health of a city and its leaders. Too often, central-city leaders and those in major institutions become embattled and defensive, fearing that they are doomed to continue fighting merely to make the best of an inexorable cycle of decline.

Evidence of dramatic improvements in even small areas of a city can have a positive impact on these leaders as well as on residents. A cautionary note is in order here: Revitalization efforts usually generate community excitement that is completely out of proportion to the achievement—spurring hopes (and bitter fears) that the entire city will soon be transformed.

INTEGRATING SCHOOLS IN REVIVING NEIGHBORHOODS

A critical limit to integration in central-city neighborhoods is lack of integrated public schools. The local schools usually enroll only poor black or Hispanic children once gentrification begins. Since most of the white newcomers with children are young professionals, the challenge is to convince them to stay and send their children to public schools.

The school problem is a major constraint on the future of urban neighborhoods. Demographic studies show that whites in their twenties are moving into cities and those in their thirties, childbearing age, are moving out in large numbers. A very high percentage of whites who do have school-age children in central cities decide that they must enroll them in the private and parochial schools that serve the majority of white students in a number of central cities.[80] A recent study of integrated neighborhoods in Chicago found few white families using public schools, and those who did attaching very great importance to school quality.[81] In a society where nine-tenths of children attend public school and where private education is very expensive, the belief that city public schools are unacceptable is obviously a serious disadvantage for the cities. The school problem helps explain why four-fifths of integrated neighborhoods are not continuing to attract sufficient whites to remain integrated and why many of those that appear relatively stable are occupied largely by temporary residents with few children in rental accommodations.[82] This is integration accomplished by a constant turnover of young whites without a lasting commitment to the neighborhood or the city.

One solution to the school problem is a good school desegregation plan. If white public school children are to be reassigned from their neighborhoods as part of a desegregation order, some can be reassigned to the minority schools in reviving neighborhoods. In a metropolitan desegregation plan, the schools in such neighborhoods can be made very similar in racial composition to all other schools in the metropolitan area. Under such plans public school students from the city are assigned to attend school in the suburbs for a good part of their school career.

This is what happened in Wilmington, Del., when a metropolitan school desegregation plan was implemented in 1978. The city had areas of severe decay but also many areas of considerable historic interest. A rehabilitation movement in some areas had failed to bring whites into public schools that were nine-tenths black. When the metropolitan desegregation plan was implemented, the city's schools were merged with those of 10 suburban districts. Thus, all of the schools became predominantly white, and all of the children were scheduled to go to school in the suburbs for nine years out of twelve.[83]

During the first year of the metropolitan plan, there was a significant drop in white enrollment in the suburbs (a normal first-year effect). There was, however, a little-noticed but very significant *rise* in white enrollment from among residents in many areas of the central city.[84] In other words, integration of central-city schools by busing in suburbanites spurred increased white enrollment from the integrated neighborhoods. Officials of the merged district report that local realtors now sometimes market housing in central-city neighborhoods on the basis of the part of the suburbs a neighborhood is paired with.[85] Homeseekers choose a convenient, historic neighborhood and still have well-integrated schools.

Where integration plans are limited to central cities, it may still be possible through special efforts to integrate the all-minority schools in reviving neighborhoods and to establish magnet schools that will attract enrollments from the newly arrived white families as well as from minority families. The 1980 St. Louis plan makes a special effort to integrate schools in reviving areas. It also promises a future exemption from busing if a significant number of whites who live in the area enroll in the local school. It discourages policies that would create an all-white community by a provision that busing must be reinstituted if the school becomes very largely white.

Without a desegregation plan, the task of integrating neighborhood schools in reviving areas presents special difficulties, but there are a few examples of success that can be models for similar communities. Reviving neighborhoods often have strong neighborhood organizations that can provide leadership. Unless there is a school strategy, the renovation process will have no positive effect on school integration and may even harm the public schools. It threatens neighborhood schools when it prices many resident families out of the area and brings in no new students.

Unless the schools can recruit newcomers, teachers will lose their jobs and schools will close.

It has been suggested that special programs in the neighbor-hood school may bring in the white children. I think it unlikely that such special programs will be offered by city school districts. In most cities undergoing large-scale rehabilitation, the public school system is largely black and Hispanic and is overburdened with responsibilities. Central-city school systems in districts where renovation is under way, such as those in Philadelphia and Washington, D.C., have few whites and little incentive to offer special programs to attract them. A city such as Boston, where special programs could ease compliance with the court order, may be an exceptional case.

Central-city school districts whose resources are growing far more slowly than their costs cannot afford new programs or new teachers. Typically, they face an annual choice about what to cut. In this climate it is unrealistic to expect the districts to come up with resources for programs to attract whites in a few schools. Black and Hispanic educators, fighting hard to address the needs of minority children, are hardly likely to divert resources to spe-cial programs for affluent whites in communities where minorities are being displaced. The rejection, by the Washington, D.C., school board, of a proposed academic high school in the Capitol Hill area is an example of this reality.[86] The politics of such deci-sions are easy to understand.

White families living in inner-city neighborhoods typically have few children. Research suggests that they share the negative per-ception of central-city school districts held by other white resi-dents.[87] In fact, their attitudes may be more negative for these reasons:

- Whites in the reviving areas are usually highly educated, rela-tively affluent, and very concerned about school quality as they perceive it.

- Unlike schools in Berkeley, Seattle, and some other cities I studied, their schools are not integrated and are usually all minor-ity, often all low-income minority.

- Since none of their reference group—other white neighbors of the same educational and economic background—use public schools, there is intense private-school interest and activity and the expectation of moving to the suburbs if public education is desired.

- There usually is a well-developed negative stereotype of the neighborhood school, virtually unchallenged in the relevant neighborhood society, that is shared by the few minority professional families participating in the renovation process.

This negative view of public education is almost always expressed as a view of the school's low educational quality. Yet there usually is no contact between local white residents and the school or its staff—its low educational quality is simply assumed. Parents rarely possess detailed knowledge of school programs. I think they are primarily aware of what their social reference groups have concluded about a school's quality and of easily available measures of student achievement. (Some cities publish school-by-school achievement data each year. Parents usually assume, incorrectly, that the data reflects the quality of the school rather than the background of the students.)

Whites in neighborhoods undergoing gentrification almost never, in my experience, say anything about the racial composition of the local school. Most are personally in favor of integration and wish to avoid any statement that could be interpreted as an expression of prejudice. Nonetheless, a root problem is that they all know the school is all-black or all-Hispanic. The vast majority will not enroll a child as an isolated white in any segregated minority school. Some middle-class minority families share the view that all segregated inner-city schools are inferior.

In order to succeed, a strategy to integrate public schools in the reviving central-city neighborhoods must explicitly attack each of the major problems. It must involve middle-class residents in the school and bring them into contact with school personnel. It must directly attack the stereotype of the inferiority of the educational program. And—most crucial—it must organize a change that will bring about substantial integration at a specified time, so that parents will face a decision about enrolling their child in an integrated school, not one in which their child would be in almost complete racial and class isolation.

This strategy was successful in one neighborhood in the Capitol Hill section of Washington, D.C.. Community newsletters about school programs, open houses at the school, and use of local organization lists to bring together a critical mass of parents led to integration of Peabody School in the fall of 1974. Integration was later expanded to include another D.C. school that merged with Peabody. Veola Jackson, the black principal who was at the center of the effort, was later given the additional assignment of developing an integrated middle school in the area.

The integration process greatly increased parent participation in the school and spurred numerous drives to raise funds for school needs. Families with children began to move into the neighborhood because of the school (which retained a black majority but was substantially integrated), and children of black middle-class families were drawn back from private schools. Showing a dramatic gain in educational performance, the public schools became a selling point in attracting families with children into the area.[88]

GUARANTEEING NEIGHBORHOOD SAFETY

The pervasive fear of crime in urban areas is a major challenge to those committed to maintaining the attractiveness and stability of integrated neighborhoods. Part of the fear of the ghetto-creation process is the fear of an increase in crime after racial change.

Attitudes of minority and white families in eight integrated neighborhoods in Chicago were analyzed in a 1980 draft report, "Crime and Urban Development," by Richard Taub and Garth Taylor of the University of Chicago. The authors concluded:

> For the white people who live in Chicago's neighborhoods, concern for one's safety in the neighborhood and the safety of one's children in school is an issue that is in many ways confounded with how one perceives and reacts to racial change in the housing market and schools in one's immediate area. . . . .
>
> By and large, our analyses show that blacks want the same neighborhood qualities as whites—low crime, low nuisance, good schools.[89]

Although most residents reported that they did not believe that crime increased when blacks began to move into a white neighborhood, a significant minority held the opposite view: about 30 per cent of whites and blacks and almost half of the Hispanics questioned said that racial change was associated with a rise in crime.[90]

Among the families interviewed, one white family in fourteen, one Hispanic family in thirteen, and one black family in ten had had a family member robbed, assaulted, or raped in the neighborhood during the previous year. When burglary and vandalism were added, a third of the whites and Hispanics and 42 per cent of black families had experienced some kind of crime during the previous twelve months. Nevertheless, few considered their neighborhoods to have "a lot" of crime by Chicago standards, and almost 30 per cent said that they had chosen their present home for safety reasons. Almost two-thirds said that they were afraid to walk alone at night in their neighborhoods. A sixth of the whites, a fifth of the Hispanics, and a third of the blacks said that they kept guns at home for protection.[91]

Obviously safety was very much on people's minds, and school safety was a major concern among those with children in public school.[92] Since the confidence of existing and potential owners and renters was vital to maintain integration, programs that increased the sense of safety in the neighborhood and in the neighborhood school were important in these communities.

The neighborhoods studied tended to be well organized. The study found some evidence that the neighborhoods with supplemental (private) security patrols experienced less street crime and disorder. Across the eight communities, 40 per cent of whites and more than half of blacks were members of local homeowner or neighborhood organizations; the number was over 70 per cent in one community.

Neighborhood organizations in such areas are both a vehicle for expressing concern about crime and a potential instrument for stimulating change. Research on apparently successful local efforts to combat crime, systematic evaluation of their claims to success, and publicity about good programs would be helpful to these communities. Crime-control programs could be made integral parts of the community development strategies in such neighborhoods.

INTEGRATING WHITE AREAS

The central problem of segregation in urban education is that the vast majority of students live in areas where there are few, if any, students of the other race. In the Chicago metropolitan area, for example, there are more than 250 totally black public schools and more than 50 black Catholic schools.[93] There are several black suburbs with black schools, but more suburbs are almost all white. Hispanics are less segregated, particularly in the suburbs, but are now finding their children more and more isolated in central-city schools. Now that the days of massive urban renewal are past, there is no substantial program for transforming and integrating ghettos and barrios. Many inner-city neighborhoods now have little appeal for anyone. They are rapidly losing population density, as minority families move farther out, and in some neighborhoods abandonment of property is widespread. Any major transformation in the most segregated areas would require resources and authority far beyond those available in urban programs even at the height of planning for the Great Society. These programs are, moreover, likely to shrink during the Reagan Administration.

Some actions can, of course, be taken. Certain neighborhoods have strong locational advantages or great capital investments from powerful institutions such as corporate headquarters, universities, and hospitals. Appropriate policies may crystallize reinvestment there. Elsewhere, cities could encourage controlled, private efforts to expand rehabilitation beyond existing focal points, but the impact would usually be small. The first priority in expanding the number of integrated areas must be a concerted effort to integrate the many segregated white areas—those from which white students must otherwise be bused when a desegregation order is handed down.

A strategy for integrating white areas involves a series of actions:

1) opening up the private market
2) improving the operation of housing subsidy programs for low-income families
3) creating regulations or incentives, or both, for mixed-use private development
4) ensuring that low-income housing is appropriately marketed
5) acting strongly against real estate discrimination and steering
6) providing pro-integration counseling
7) (optional) designing subsidies for individual families or realtors and rental agents, or both, to encourage integrative moves

One element of the strategy can be school desegregation plans that reward integrated communities.

There is a widespread belief in the country today that housing discrimination is a thing of the past for blacks and Hispanics with money enough to purchase housing on the private market. Public opinion polls show that the majority of whites say they would have no objection to a black neighbor of similar status. Most people believe that the real estate market is open.[94] Congress decided in late 1980 that a fair-housing enforcement bill was unnecessary. Realtors and school statistics show a rapid increase in the number of black and brown suburbanites. An increasing number of white suburbanites report that at least one black family lives nearby. Surveys show a very strong black preference for living in integrated rather than all-black areas. Typically, less than a tenth of blacks express a preference for an all-black community.[95]

Still, there is virtually no improvement in the level of integration in urban neighborhood schools after twelve years of fair housing. There are a few blacks and a few more Hispanics in a number of formerly all-white suburbs, but the great majority of non-white middle-class families are still moving into segregated or rapidly changing neighborhoods. There are more black suburbanites primarily because, in a number of cities, ghettos have expanded beyond the city line and into the inner suburbs.

Demographers, who have studied distribution of people in metropolitan areas by race and income, report that income differences do not explain the current level of black segregation. The average poor white lives in an area with more middle-class families than the average middle-class black. If blacks were distributed around metropolitan areas by income in the same way whites with similar incomes are distributed, a large majority would live in predominantly white suburbs.[96]

Fair-housing enforcement is obviously a key problem. Increasing its effectiveness will require:

- authority—a law with significant power
- capacity—sufficient resources to publicize the law and investigate violations
- an enforcement strategy
- stronger penalties for violators
- increased minority participation in the real-estate business

The federal fair-housing law provides no administrative enforcement powers for HUD. Reliance on Justice Department litigation has proved completely unworkable, producing long delays in the few cases litigated each year. Defeat of the 1980 federal fair-housing bill means that the problem will continue. Many state and local agencies are similarly enfeebled.[97]

Federal, state, and local fair-housing enforcement agencies have small staffs that usually receive no adequate training. Too often federal administrations treat these agencies as administrative ghettos—plums for politically loyal minority supporters, to be staffed by minority officials without training. Thus, one of our society's most difficult administrative tasks—changing the behavior of profoundly discriminatory private institutions through a weak and complex enforcement process—is treated as if it requires no special skills. Yet effective civil rights enforcement requires a good working knowledge both of civil rights law and the substantive policy area, as well as persistence and skill in raising issues that agencies find it easier to ignore.

The equal-opportunity agencies rarely have prestige or access to the top levels of the executive branch. Top officials assume that they have nothing to contribute to the substantive policy decisions that may have much greater consequences for minority families than civil rights enforcement efforts. A change in housing finance policy can, for example, have a considerable impact on residential integration. Recognizing the importance of these agencies and increasing the size and training of their staffs are essential if there is to be serious fair-housing enforcement.

Seldom is there any actual penalty for violating the law against housing discrimination. Only a small number of cases are reported, and a small fraction of those are successfully resolved. Often the process takes so long that by the time the case is concluded the victim has settled elsewhere. For the law to have significant impact, it is necessary to increase the probability that a violator will be caught and to raise the penalty for those who are caught. The former requires an adequate, well-trained staff. The latter requires an increase in financial penalties and suspension of violators from real estate practice.

Enforcement resources of civil rights agencies are not expanding, even though their responsibilities have been extended in many directions. This means shrinking resources for work on problems of racial segregation in housing. Most cases end without an award of significant cash damages—though there are some dramatic exceptions—and real estate licenses are seldom suspended even temporarily. State and local officials and private agencies seriously concerned about housing opportunities should consider monitoring and exposing local discrimination and increasing penalties for violations.[98]

Housing discrimination is simply not considered a serious crime. To corroborate this statement, you need only compare the sanctions for housing discrimination with those for violating a law the government does take seriously—for example, draft registration or income tax. If action against housing discrimination is seen for what it is—an important part of the answer to the question whether we can build an interracial society in the U.S.—it is clear that the present enforcement process is inexcusably weak.

The connection between school desegregation and stronger fair-housing laws was recognized in Ohio. After the state's largest cities were sued by the NAACP, a state legislative committee created to explore alternatives to busing recommended, as a priority, putting some teeth in fair-housing enforcement. Although the legislature wished to avoid involvement with the politically controversial issues of school integration, in 1979 it did approve tougher fair-housing enforcement, including license-revocation for guilty realtors. Considering the current lack of enthusiasm for tougher civil rights laws, Ohio's 1979 decision to support fair-housing enforcement as a possible long-term alternative to busing may have been crucially important.[99]

Only one significant force in the housing market has a strong and immediate vested interest in widening housing opportunities for minority families—the minority brokers. Many minority families prefer—and are prepared to pay a premium for—high-quality, low-crime neighborhoods with good public schools. Minority brokers rarely get white clients, but they have black and Hispanic clients who want housing outside minority areas. If they can get the listings, they can make money.

Integrated neighborhoods offer minority brokers almost the only opportunity they have to obtain listings for their clients outside the ghetto or barrio. A Chicago NAACP leader—a broker living in an integrated South Side neighborhood—was bitterly critical of housing stabilization efforts designed to keep whites moving in and thus prevent ghettoization. Many of his clients, he said, were prepared to pay $10,000 more for a house in an integrated area than for a similar one elsewhere, but he could not get listings.[100] They are usually given to minority brokers only after homeowners have decided that it will be impossible to obtain a white buyer at their desired price. Then minority brokers are often blamed as the agents of resegregation.

It would be much better, of course, for the brokers, their clients, and the cause of housing integration if the minority brokers had access to all listings. More areas would become integrated and less demand would be focused on a few integrated areas wishing to stabilize. The goals of increasing the number of minority brokers and increasing the employment of minorities in large white-owned real estate offices are extremely important. Similar attention must be given to staffing sales and rental offices run by developers and landlords.

Given that 98 per cent of U.S. housing is in the private market, it is of the greatest importance that the one part of the market with the strongest reason to support vigorous expansion of minority housing opportunities be offered every possible assistance. The practice of dividing metropolitan areas into a number of separate real estate boards, with separate multiple-listing services, and allowing minority brokers membership only in the central-city boards, can make the minority brokers instruments of the ghetto-creation process. Civil rights enforcement officials and real estate licensing agencies should give high priority to increasing employment of blacks and Hispanics in all sectors of the industry, including those in all-white areas.

DEVELOPING ENFORCEMENT STRATEGIES

State and local civil rights agencies usually devote all of their meager resources to complaint processing. If you visit their offices you find small staffs months behind in processing complaint forms. Often the same staffs have jurisdiction over job discrimination, community-relations problems, and other civil rights activities.

In recent years the responsibilities of civil rights agencies have been expanded far beyond traditional racial issues. There is legislation against sex discrimination, against age discrimination, against discrimination toward handicapped or gay people. Some agencies receive more complaints of sex discrimination than of race discrimination.[101] Educated middle-class women are more likely than poor blacks or Latinos to know about the law and understand bureaucratic processes. Usually, far more complaints are filed on job discrimination than on housing problems. Poorly informed victims and ineffective enforcement serve to minimize complaints.[102] Then, completing a vicious circle, the small number of complaints leads to minimal enforcement.

Civil rights agencies should develop the capacity to advise other federal, state, and local agencies. They could, for example, provide advice and assistance to real estate licensing agencies, state and local housing authorities, and also transportation and highway planners and other officials who have a great influence on housing segregation but rarely consider the issue. Upgrading the analytic capacity of civil rights staffs so that they could participate in policy development and policy evaluation would be highly useful. Organized information and advice on housing patterns could aid development of better school desegregation plans.

HOUSING COUNSELING CENTERS

During the early 1970s a number of housing counseling centers were established, often with assistance from the Office of Economic Opportunity or the Ford Foundation, to work on opening up segregated white areas for minority families with enough money to buy or rent homes there. The idea was to try to break the cycle of segregation at two points: first, by letting minority families know about the full range of available housing, and second, by providing assistance against discrimination in the new setting. Sometimes the housing counseling centers had access to special funds—small mortgage-subsidy funds—to help families over the financial barrier of buying their first suburban home.

Some of those centers are now defunct or engaged in other

work. Foundation interest has diminished, government interest never developed on a substantial scale, and many of the most committed staff members have gone elsewhere. The Denver center, for example, no longer exists. Many people claim that, after all, blacks and Hispanics can now move wherever they want. Anyway, they say, perhaps it is wrong to commit resources to speeding the migration of minority leaders from the community at a time of very great problems for blacks and Hispanics.

The attack on organized efforts for integration from some black leaders has an intriguing quality. Black politicians, including East St. Louis Mayor Carl Officer, for example, joined a successful attack on proposed mobility program in the suburbs of St. Louis, arguing that it would weaken the base of black political power. If you accept the research showing that black segregation is involuntary and that a great many blacks would prefer to move away from the heart of the ghetto, these political leaders are actually saying that government should not take modest steps to open up the possibility of integration for a small number of blacks who would prefer it. They are saying that blacks should be forced to remain to support the political power of black officials. Even this political power is a sometime thing. East St. Louis went bankrupt in December 1980 and was unable to pay the salaries of its black employees. The city to which blacks were confined had not a single department store or theater and was losing its last substantial employers. Its school system was such a disgrace that the state of Illinois had it in receivership for several years.[103] The mayor found it necessary to carry a gun in his city.

The proposition that black or Hispanic families should be confined as part of a racial group to provide a political power base for public officials who happen to come from that group is fundamentally wrong in my view and that of the integration movement. If we continue to slam the door of opportunity on those very non-white families who are working most diligently to escape from conditions no white American would tolerate, we deserve and can expect deep disaffection. These families have the right to nothing less than a real opportunity to decide where they want to live. That opportunity is not now available. Even if everything suggested here is done, severe housing segregation is likely to be a problem for a long time to come.

In most of the communities I studied for this report, there was no housing counseling center working on private market integration. The kind of organized white liberal support for such efforts that was available in the late 1960s is usually lacking today. Certain counseling efforts have managed to survive and play a useful role, sometimes with the support of enlightened self-interest from integrated communities fighting the forces of resegregation. The Cuyahoga Plan, in metropolitan Cleveland, for example, operates on a substantial scale, has achieved considerable financial security, and has played a significant role in a remarkable middle-class black migration from the central city. The plan continually advertises for minority clients, offers professional counseling, takes people out to look at neighborhoods, conducts testing, and maintains relationships with real estate brokers sympathetic to its goals. The organization monitors very closely the racial trends in its metropolitan area.[104] It has provided an invaluable service in an urban community with a tradition of poor race relations. There are similar efforts in Chicago and a few other communities.

In much of the country, however, no significant attempt is being made to accomplish any voluntary residential (and thus school) integration that can be accomplished through the private market. Those who denounce busing should not be surprised that so much of it is needed to integrate schools—we are not really trying to integrate neighborhoods. Housing centers with well-trained and committed staffs are needed in every metropolitan area, if there is to be any approach to equal opportunity. Federal grants, private foundations, and local community development budgets should give this project a high priority.

HOUSING SUBSIDIES AND INTEGRATION OF WHITE AREAS
You might reasonably assume that if middle-class black and Hispanic families are excluded from white areas, it would be virtually impossible to obtain access for subsidized housing for minority families. After all, these families would not only have to confront racial prejudice but also a strong preference for economic homogeneity and a strong disapproval of the life style of many subsidized housing tenants—unwed mothers with small children living on welfare payments. You need only look at the location of subsidized housing projects in any major city to realize that local public officials almost always conclude that such families should live in segregated areas.

An important experiment in Louisville shows that housing subsidy programs may hold far more potential for residential integration (and school integration) than was previously believed. This impression is reinforced by evidence from a court-ordered effort to move some Chicago public housing tenants to the suburbs. Together with experience in metropolitan Baltimore, these programs show that there are low-income black families ready to move if they are given appropriate help, and that their experience is usually highly positive.

The Louisville experiment is a simple test of black interest in moving outside the ghetto and of the use of housing policy to relieve school segregation. Without any decision by federal or local housing officials, the Kentucky Human Rights Commission put a woman to work showing black families that were receiving Section 8 rent-subsidy certificates the housing available in white sections of the metropolitan area. About half have chosen to move there. Under the Louisville court order, the move immediately exempts their children from busing.[105] This has occurred in a community where there was very high racial tension when the court order was first implemented five years ago.

Little research has been done in Louisville, but we know a good deal about the motivations and experiences of hundreds of Chicago families participating in similar moves under the provisions of a court-ordered plan for housing desegregation. The plan was implemented in the late 1970s in the nation's most segregated large metropolitan area.

POOR BLACKS IN THE CHICAGO SUBURBS

One of two types of racial change that occurred previously in Chicago was outward movement of middle-class black families in search of better schools, housing, and neighborhoods. The other type was expansion of small pockets of black settlement in the suburbs. Most middle-class families moved relatively short distances outside all-black communities, and most were resegregated in the suburban communities to which they moved. Relatively few families, including some black professionals, moved to distant white communities.

In 1976 the courts found both the city of Chicago and the federal government guilty of unconstitutional segregation in the development of Chicago's vast high-rise public housing projects.[106] These projects were built after World War II in spite of early warnings that they would not provide fit environments for children. But white aldermen had vetoed cheaper sites in the outlying areas of the city where low-density family construction within the federal government's per-unit-cost ceiling would have been possible. The projects were built on slum sites after thousands of black housing units had been destroyed to create them.[107] The children in the projects, of course, were faced with segregated schools from the outset.

The Supreme Court's order in 1976 initiated negotiations between HUD and civil rights lawyers that produced a plan giving Chicago housing-project tenants and those on public-housing waiting lists the opportunity to live in integrated areas. HUD contracted for administration of the program with the Leadership Council of Metropolitan Open Communities, the local fair-housing organization created in the mid-1960s in response to violence against Martin Luther King's open-housing marches in Chicago. After a decade of struggle, the Leadership Council had an opportunity to test the workability of its vision of suburbs open to victims of the most intense inner-city segregation.

Initiating the change—finding cooperative landlords in the suburbs and recruiting the first black pioneers—was very difficult. The units found were scattered in many suburbs, requiring an average move of more than 20 miles.[108] Many experts and community leaders had long argued that poor black people would not want to leave their neighborhoods and friends for a distant white area with poor public transit.

Progress was slow at first. During the first 2½ years, 22,000 families were notified of the program, about 1,800 came to briefings, 1,100 were visited at home by the Leadership Council, 970 visited apartments, and 455 families moved in.[109]

Those that did move were interviewed in early 1979 by University of Michigan researchers. More than nine-tenths of the families were black, 85 per cent were headed by women, and two-thirds came directly from the Chicago projects. The average family comprised two children and an unemployed parent. Many (43 per cent) had initial doubts about moving, worrying especially about discrimination, unfamiliarity, and poor public transportation. (A comparable group of families that moved to subsidized housing within the city had a different basic fear—crime.)[110]

The new suburbanites reported that their hopes for the suburbs had been largely fulfilled and their fears dissipated. More than four in five thought their new neighborhood was better. Eighty-five per cent said that housing quality, good public schools, and freedom from crime had been their most important reasons for moving.[111]

Five out of six of those who moved said that the availability of good schools was a very important consideration, and more than two-thirds thought the suburban schools were actually better. About a fourth said that racial integration was very important to their decision to move, and another fifth said it was somewhat important.[112]

The families interviewed found suburban life better than they had expected. They usually emphasized the traditional lures of suburbia in describing their new community: They said they liked best the privacy, quiet, space, and good public services. Most reported that the schools were better and the neighbors friendlier than they had foreseen. About two-thirds "reported almost every problem to be less serious than it was in their old neighborhood."[113]

Transportation was a problem. About an eighth of those who moved (compared with a fourteenth of those who remained in the city) said that their home was far from their job. In a relatively short time, however, most of the parents who were working or going to school were working or being educated in suburban location. Commuting members of families in the suburbs spent an average of thirty-seven minutes traveling to work. Nonparticipants, who remained in the city and worked, spent an average of thirty-eight minutes traveling to work.[114] Those in the suburbs who had to go to welfare offices said that it was harder to get there but the service was better.

The families that had moved viewed the efforts of housing counselors very positively. Ninety-three per cent said they had been helpful, The program was rapidly growing in 1980, having more than doubled at 1,000 families.[115]

SCATTERED-SITE HOUSING

The most obvious civil rights violations in the administration of housing programs have occurred in site selection, tenant-assignment policies, and practices of subsidized housing programs. Courts have repeatedly held that it is illegal to use public funds to build segregated housing. These decisions have produced large confrontations between the courts, local housing authorities and city councils, and the federal government in such cities as Chicago and Philadelphia. Official decisions that segregate residential patterns can only increase segregation in schools. Such evidence is often developed in school cases as part of the proof that school segregation is not accidental but is the result, in good measure, of a complex set of official decisions.

If some housing location and tenanting decisions can intensify school segregation, other housing decisions can help. Under the spur of court decisions, the 1964 Civil Rights Act, the 1968 Fair Housing Law, and the provision of the Community Development Act calling for "spatial deconcentration" of the poor, HUD has made some efforts to improve regulations governing local programs. The issue has proved extremely difficult, however. A successful scattered-site policy requires cooperation from local governments concerned and from private developers that actually build most subsidized housing. At the neighborhood level, subsidized housing is often strongly resisted. Developers do not like to get caught in political cross fire over the controversial family projects. Since local resistance is strong and HUD has rarely used its most powerful sanction—cutoff of federal aid funds—an impasse has frequently been reached. Very rarely have housing plans been linked with school desegregation.

HUD's most important effort has been to develop an approach to determine the metropolitan need for subsidized housing through Areawide Housing Opportunity Programs (AHOPs). An AHOP analyzes total housing needs and allocates responsibility for building subsidized units among the participating jurisdictions. Most of the cities I visited for this study—Minneapolis, Seattle, Denver, Wilmington, Louisville, Charlotte, and St. Petersburg—are among the metropolitan areas with HUD-approved AHOPs. In some of these metropolitan areas, a very substantial fraction of the subsidized housing is being built in the suburbs. Minneapolis-St. Paul and Seattle, for example, have excellent records in this respect. Both have relatively small metropolitan minority populations but substantial minority school enrollment in the central city.

In areas with strong AHOPs and small minority populations, a plan to use the scattered housing to promote integration could have a significant impact on the success of the school desegregation plan. Denver already has a 58 per cent minority, central-city district attempting to stabilize a desegregation plan limited to the central city. The city contains only one-eighth of the Anglo students in the metropolitan region.[116] Seattle and Minneapolis have large and increasing minority enrollments, with desegregation plans limited to the city, and both are surrounded by rapidly growing suburbs with very few minority families.[117]

AHOPs assume that if housing is scattered it will be integrated. They assume, in other words, that the race problem is actually an economic problem. They have learned none of the lessons—available in the report of a study by the U.S. Commission on Civil Rights—from the housing subsidy programs of the early 1970s. The commission found that subsidized units in white areas usually went to low-income whites, some of whom had moved from integrated areas, and subsidized units in minority or integrated areas were left for minorities.[118] Thus, a subsidy program that ignores race can easily subsidize both white flight and creation of ghettos from integrated neighborhoods.

Usually, AHOPs lack the counseling effort that would make them a strategy for integration, and they seldom encourage substantial transfer of minority families across jurisdictional lines to white areas. Even in areas with highly regarded AHOP programs, such as Minneapolis and Seattle, the responsible officials said that there was no effort to encourage racial integration.[119] The offices did not even keep track of placement by race.

Seattle, for example, had an interjurisdictional agreement to permit the use of Section 8 subsidy certificates in any part of the metropolitan area. This looked, on paper, like a major advance, and substantial new construction of subsidized housing was under way in the suburbs. There was no machinery, however, to encourage transfers to the suburbs and almost none took place. Fewer than ten people had crossed jurisdictional lines by January 1980, and housing officials thought that some of these transfers were the accidental result of going into the wrong office to make an application.[120]

In Minneapolis officials of the Metropolitan Council said that there was no effort to use the program for racial integration, no counseling, and no link with the public schools. Their impression was that the minority population of the Twin City region was so small that they could safely ignore the issue.[121] (Minneapolis school officials did not share this perspective.) A study of selected U.S. metropolitan areas by Richard Fleisher, now at Fordham University, reported that scattered-site suburban housing usually went to whites.[122] Much of the subsidized housing built in the suburbs of Denver, Phoenix, and Columbus, Ohio, was rented to whites, according to a 1981 study for HUD.[123]

The problem here is not the AHOP concept or the allocation of extra units to metropolitan areas that adopt AHOPs. It is that one more component is essential to convert them into programs that would assist in school desegregation. AHOP regulations must be revised to require outreach and counseling for minority tenants and to set integration goals for developers of the subsidized housing. HUD should make these stipulations a part of any AHOP.

MIXED-INCOME REQUIREMENTS

Some governmental organizations have responded to the critical shortage of subsidized housing, and the overwhelming dominance of the private sector, by reaching the conclusion that the most important necessity is to incorporate an element of subsidized housing in the major private-market developments. This conclusion is based on the premise that there is so much economic incentive to undertake large subdivisions in desirable areas, when the market is strong, that developers would be willing to include a relatively small proportion of subsidized units. An incentive might be given, in the form of permission for denser development—a very important consideration in areas of extremely high land costs. A local ordinance along these lines, requiring construction of 15 per cent low- and moderate-income housing in all subdivisions of more than 50 units, has been in operation for years in Montgomery County, Md., one of the nation's wealthiest suburban counties.[124]

Similar requirements in parts of Orange County, the most affluent portion of southern California, have produced a significant number of housing units.[125] In San Francisco, developers of high-rise housing receive incentives for including units for low- and moderate-income tenants. The California Coastal Commission, which controls development in the coastal region, has adopted an "incentive system" in processing development requests. This system had produced 600 units of low- and moderate-income housing in extremely desirable areas by mid-1980. An additional 3,500 units had been approved and were in the pipeline.

Experience with hundreds of applications had convinced a commission expert that "direct, on-site inclusion of approximately 25 per cent of a project as affordable housing is feasible in most projects of 16 units or greater." The diversity of the housing had not damaged its marketing prospects and had not prevented financing commitments from the area's leading institutions.[126] Given the probability that funds for construction of new subsidized housing will shrink in coming years, this is an important policy initiative. Once again, however, there is no assurance that this approach will aid integration unless a conscious effort is made to do so.

PLANNED INTEGRATION EFFORTS

Some significant efforts have been made to plan affirmatively for integration—with owners, developers, or government agencies setting goals for integrating of specific projects or neighborhoods. Goals are set for development in areas that do not have a sizable minority population at the outset and would not normally increase it without special efforts. Among the early efforts of this sort in private projects were those sponsored during the 1960s by M-REIT, a pro-integration investment trust operating in several cities. Perhaps the largest and most successful was the planned integration of the new town of Columbia, Md., between

Washington and Baltimore. Columbia opened with and has retained substantial integration of both neighborhoods and schools.[127] It shows that there is a substantial black market for housing in distant suburban areas and that whites will continue to move to and bid up housing prices in an area where integration is perceived to be stable.

The only similar effort I encountered during this research was in Michigan. One of the goals specified in the Ann Arbor Housing Assistance Plan for the 1980 fiscal year is to "provide assisted housing in locations which promote racial balance in the school system."[128] A local project playing a positive role in this effort is a 300-unit development, in a desirable section of the city, that mixes 60 per cent market-rate units with 40 per cent assisted units. It has a successful affirmative marketing plan that has attracted black families.[129]

The key promoter of the complex was the Michigan State Housing Development Authority, which had helped in the production of 19,000 low- and moderate-income rental units across Michigan. The state agency establishes integration goals for each project and directs developers to hold units off the market, if necessary, to meet the goals. The agency has had considerable success in integrating its projects, except in Detroit, where it has been unable to attract whites.[130]

Policies of this sort could be very important, particularly in areas of extensive new development. Sunbelt cities still experiencing massive growth have an opportunity to avoid the mistakes of older cities as they double or triple their size in the next generation. The Michigan agency's policy requires:

> . . . an active, aggressive and affirmative approach to the soliciting of eligible buyers and renters from all racial and ethnic groups . . . by all sponsors and marketing agents associated with developments financed in part or in total by the Authority. . . . Where it will take a special effort to inform minority group persons of the existence of and attract them to a development, that effort must be made. On the other hand, when it will take such an effort to inform and attract non-minority persons to a development, a special effort must also be made. The absence of persons from either minority or non-minority backgrounds in a development will be considered prima facie evidence of discrimination on the part of those persons responsible for the marketing of development and corrective actions must be taken.[131]

SITE-SELECTION TIED TO SCHOOL DESEGREGATION
The idea of examining school desegregation implications in

preparing new housing proposals seems to be most fully developed in Charlotte, N.C. In 1974–1975, the city adopted policies on tenant integration and on selection of future sites for subsidized housing construction. When city officials went around to neighborhood meetings in 1975 to try to sell the concept of scattered-site subsidized projects, the school connection was emphasized, as reflected in the *Charlotte Observer:*

> . . . the presentation, flashing photos of yellow school buses, hailed the concept of scattered public housing as a beginning of a solution to the problem of crosstown busing of public school students, which the federal court has mandated in a community of segregated housing patterns.
>
> The authority is hoping that people prefer integrated neighborhoods to busing, an idea that has been given a lot of lip service in recent years but has never been tested.[132]

The Charlotte city council unanimously adopted a policy of building all family housing on low-density, scattered sites and trying to integrate the resulting projects. In the city's housing plan, white neighborhoods in many portions of the city were targeted for relatively small, low-density developments. At this point the city ran into serious problems with the HUD area office, according to several city officials. The HUD office opposed the exclusion of large portions of the city and refused to approve the costs of some sites in the expensive white areas of the city. Charlotte was threatened with a cutoff of HUD funds, but the problems were eventually negotiated. In 1979 the first scattered-site units were completed and opened.[133] A number of Charlotte officials felt that the HUD field office had been the most important obstacle to their plan.

All participants in Charlotte emphasized that the housing construction policy in itself would not make a vast difference. The number of units built each year was small, and the subsidized share of the total housing market was less than 5 per cent. Even if everything was done right, it would take years for the direct impact to be large. (We do not know whether moving a few blacks to various areas through subsidy programs will have a broader effect outside those programs.) The housing authorities, at least, were acting in a way that helped rather than hurt school desegregation. Local officials recognized that school officials had a strong and legitimate right to be consulted in all major housing decisions. Charlotte was the only jurisdiction I visited where both planners and school officials mentioned that school integration considerations were a significant concern in the city's planning process.[134]

Some of Charlotte's inner-city neighborhoods were being re-
vived. Since their public schools were already integrated, new
families were inclined to use them. Although neither the court
order nor the school board had a policy of exempting of integrated neighborhoods, some ad hoc exemptions had been made. A
continuation of the back-to-the-city trend combined with a
Louisville-style policy could facilitate further progress. Charlotte,
which showed unusual sensitivity to the site issue, could build on
the experience of other cities on such dimensions as exemption of
integrated neighborhoods from busing and the provision of integration counseling in the existing Section 8 program.

What Are the Policy Options?

This project was both exciting and frustrating, in that it demonstrated very widespread interest in better policy coordination but revealed no single policy likely to solve the problem. School and housing policies interact at many levels, and potential policy changes involve many agencies and interests. Intriguing and important experiments on specific aspects of the problem are under way in various cities, but no strategy has been fully articulated. Comprehensive approaches could be formulated only if many officials understood the interaction of school and housing changes and committed their organizations to integration as a high priority. While this may be an ultimate goal, it is not likely to be realized in any major city in the near future.

There are a number of smaller policy changes that could be profitably pursued by various agencies in cities across the country. Approaches that proved workable could be summarized and evaluated promptly, and the results communicated to the relevant national organizations. They might well be tried elsewhere, particularly if they are advocated by grant-making and enforcement agencies. Individual policy initiatives on a complex multidimensional problem may make an important contribution, but their effect may be difficult to discern clearly in the short run. Simultaneous implementation of a number of mutually supportive policies in one or two large cities would be very valuable. Perhaps these policies could be explicitly tied to the long-term goal of cutting school busing by increasing integrated neighborhood schools.

A school district would be the logical organization to raise such an issue, particularly if it could obtain the necessary expertise on the implications of housing decisions for its plans. Persuading the other major institutions to undertake difficult new responsibilities in pursuit of the long-term advantage of the total community would not be easy. But if a comprehensive approach were adopted, the probability would be much greater that a significant positive effect on school and housing segregation could be achieved in the foreseeable future. Some combination of these approaches would perhaps be optimal.

TEN PRIORITIES

The total U.S. experience to date shows that, whatever approach is taken in a given community, a number of ideas are available that could move policy beyond incoherent and self-defeating attacks on the issues. This experience indicates that, if there is a strong desire on the part of the appropriate agencies to make progress toward greater integration, some relatively straightforward procedures would yield much better results. I suggest these ten priorities:

1) **Focusing on the Issue.** One of the most surprising findings of this study was that in spite of the almost universal comment that "the real problem is housing," most cities with busing plans had made no serious analysis of possible housing strategies, or of possible problems caused by existing housing strategies.

Even public school officials with the strongest vested interest in these questions had seldom thought through policy issues involved in a coordinated strategy of school and housing desegregation. School boards had to deal with the consequences of changes in housing, but they rarely understood the housing policies that produced the problem. Housing officials rarely considered the issue in any way. During a period when there has been little national leadership and little public interest in integration, the question of desegregation has virtually disappeared from the public agenda except in cities with major court battles. Before intelligent action can be taken on complex issues, the problems must be understood and the choices publicized. Many communities are totally unaware of the nature or implications of current local trends.

Important parts of any comprehensive strategy would be summarizing the school and housing statistics and trends, briefing the full spectrum of community leaders, and providing comprehensible materials to the public and the mass media. Perhaps the best way to begin would be with one-day civic conferences requested by the school boards and organized by school, housing, and civil rights agencies in cooperation with the relevant federal officials and researchers. Such a conference was organized with HUD sponsorship in Denver in January 1981. Other recent conferences, in Milwaukee, Pittsburgh, and Los Angeles, have also addressed the issue.

**2) Developing Appropriate Housing Plans Before School De-
segregation Is Ordered.** In a number of urban areas, there is a
real possibility of court-ordered school desegregation within a
single system or at the metropolitan level. It will be some time,
however, before plans for these areas are formulated. During the
years of investigation and litigation, major steps could be taken,
through housing policy, to increase the number of integrated
neighborhoods that would be exempted from a busing plan. The
suburbs of Indianapolis face a metropolitan plan next year. The
suburbs of Cleveland, St. Louis, and Cincinnati, and perhaps Milwaukee and Kansas City, may well be entering long legal battles
over the issue in the near future. The Justice Department has
been attempting to initiate a metropolitan case in Houston and in
Charleston, S.C.

Typically, no consideration is given to steps to diminish the
burden on the school plan while the legal struggle is under way.
Housing strategies, devised during this process, could be tied to
the promise of an exemption from any order that might be
handed down. In Phoenix, Ariz., the city's Human Relations Division, along with several housing agencies and community development organizations, was discussing the possibility of such an
approach during 1980 as the Justice Department was investigating
schools and housing in the Phoenix metropolitan area.

Cities, especially growing cities, face large choices about the
future, as do suburbs involved in metropolitan cases. There has
never been a concerted housing policy effort at this stage. It could
be part of a vastly more rational local approach to school litigation. If it worked somewhere, it would certainly attract a great
deal of national attention. Local politicians assailing busing could
be shown a concrete example of a community that had cut busing
during litigation through a housing strategy.

**3) Developing School Desegregation Plans More Likely to
Encourage and Reward Housing Desegregation.** Most court orders and state-imposed school desegregation plans are designed
without any attention to housing issues or any provision for demographic change. Many plans bus children out of integrated
neighborhoods. Experience in the cities I examined suggests that
a plan fostering residential integration should:

• exempt stably integrated neighborhoods from busing

• assist neighborhoods that become integrated with supportive
community development policies

- exempt individual students from busing if they are making integration moves and if these are compatible with the plan's basic approach
- be designed with an awareness of demographic trends and impose on the school board a continuing obligation to maintain integration
- prohibit governmental housing decisions that resegregate integrated schools

Coordinated policies are most likely to be successful where the school plan includes as much as possible of the housing market area, and where explicit provisions require coordination.

There is an urgent need to bring these issues to the litigators and judges who shape school cases in the courts, and to the administrators who enforce civil rights policies for state and federal agencies. The most useful approaches might be conferences with participants in school cases, and fully developed legal and social-science articles in important law journals and education publications. If the issues in desegregation remedies are framed, from the beginning, in terms of the dynamics of metropolitan racial change, the plans are likely to be far more effective than those based merely on reassigning students who happen to be in specific schools during a given year.

4) Obtaining Housing Expertise for School Districts. Although school officials in districts with desegregation orders strongly approved the idea that housing decisions should support desegregation, none of those I interviewed had much specific knowledge of local housing programs. Big-city systems need a trained staff member whose job includes monitoring housing and development decisions, explaining their implications to top district officials, and forcefully expressing the position of the school authorities on proposals that would undermine the school desegregation plan. Should consultation fail and litigation become necessary, this staff member would be an important resource.

School districts under court orders are the only major institutions in big cities with a strong vested interest in increasing residential integration. When residential segregation expands, school authorities must either implement controversial changes in their plan or see rapid resegregation of schools integrated at great social cost. Districts should consider temporarily hiring an urban planner or housing expert to work in the superintendent's office, or a temporary exchange of personnel with housing or planning agencies.

5) Attacking Real-Estate Stereotypes About Integrated Schools.
In metropolitan areas that have desegregation plans in the
central-city school district or a few suburban districts, but also
have many other districts with virtually all white students, it is
clear that white homeseekers are steered toward areas with white
schools and away from those with integrated schools. The real
estate market reflects prejudice toward both minority students
and neighborhoods and skepticism that integration can last. It
also reflects the strong conviction that schools in the affluent white
suburbs are best. Urban school districts with desegregation plans
limited to the central city have failed to recognize the severity of
this problem. They need to devise public-relations strategies and
widely publicized special programs to reach realtors and buyers
and counter the stereotypes. Districts should establish information and recruitment centers where families could obtain information about the schools and their new programs. The centers
should welcome visits, by families seeking housing, to specified
schools in the district. Integrated school districts in segregated
metropolitan areas must successfully assail stereotypes or be severely damaged by them.

**6) Housing Counseling: Integrating White Areas, Stabilizing
Integrated Areas.** Expanding segregation and feeding on the vicious circle of the ghetto-creation process remains the basic social
reality in most urban centers. Powerful intervention in the housing market is essential if there is to be significant residential integration. The most important intervention identified in this study
is direct, individual contact and assistance to minority and white
families seeking homes. Without this intervention the probability
is very high that their moves will contribute to segregation and
that integrated areas will resegregate. Minority families in subsidized housing and those with the income to buy or rent in the
private market need such assistance.

Low-income minority families have less knowledge of white
neighborhoods and housing choices than have whites. Many do
not even know their right to freely choose housing without threat
of discrimination. Unless a special effort is made by housing officials, these minority families are very likely to end up in segregated neighborhoods with segregated schools. Public funds will be
required to bus their children to integrated schools and to bus
more white children into their neighborhoods. Housing
counseling experiments in Louisville, Chicago, and Baltimore
have revealed among black families a strong interest in living in

predominantly white areas when they are shown housing there. Housing counseling aimed at genuine choice should be a part of all local Section 8 programs. Certainly it should be required when a metropolitan area is receiving HUD incentive funds for its Areawide Housing Opportunity Plan.

Counseling is just as important in the private market, given the continuing high levels of residential segregation, the strong minority preference for integrated neighborhoods, and the steering of minority housing demand into already integrated areas where it can produce resegregation. Blacks and Hispanics with an interest in housing outside the ghetto or barrio often look first to nearby neighborhoods that appear to be integrated. (This is understandable, because they know people in the neighborhoods. In fact, however, such neighborhoods are often going through rapid racial transition.)

After the riots of the 1960s and the fair-housing demonstrations led by Martin Luther King and other civil rights leaders, considerable support for fair-housing centers came from the Office of Economic Opportunity, local businesses and governments, and private foundations. Some of these centers had an explicit commitment to open up suburban housing for blacks. Some centers continue to operate and have now developed effective techniques to aid middle-class minority families. Elsewhere the effort was plagued by declining civil rights commitment, the shutdown of the War on Poverty, division on integration policies in some black organizations, and new agendas in the private foundations. Housing counseling centers—using trained professionals—should be maintained on a long-term basis as a vital part of an urban integration policy.

7) Integrating Schools in Reviving City Neighborhoods. Whites are now returning to some newly fashionable black or brown inner-city neighborhoods. Usually the newcomers do not have school-age children. Often the neighborhoods have all-minority public schools, which lose enrollment as middle-class whites replace some of the lower-income minority families. These neighborhoods must offer good-quality, well-integrated schools if significant numbers of white (and minority) middle-class families with children are to make a permanent commitment to the city.

Most reviving areas have strong neighborhood organizations that fight against possible adverse zoning decisions, demand police protection and other city services, and support historic preservation. The new young professionals provide a reservoir of talent and influence for change. Experiments supported by the federal Department of Education or by private foundations, local community development agencies, or school districts should tap these community resources to create strong, well-integrated schools.

Small investments of time and money, spent in organizing the community and training community leaders and school principals and staffs, could produce models of successful neighborhood-level school integration. Such successes would deal with the most important constraint on family settlement in renovated housing and would eventually move toward real integration.

Experiments should focus initially on elementary schools and should attempt to organize simultaneous entry of a number of white families. (Whites are rarely willing to enroll their children as isolated individuals in virtually all-minority schools.) To succeed, the effort will probably require organizing and recruiting of families, a positive atmosphere and educational reforms in the school, and very active use of neighborhood communications channels for a direct attack on negative stereotypes about the school. Relatively small grants to a neighborhood organization and the school could be invaluable in this process. Preconditions for such grants should be:

- substantial residential integration
- a major neighborhood organization committed to the goal
- a school principal who supports integration and is willing to share power with parents

When success is achieved in one neighborhood, the process should be documented, and small grants and training should be offered to other neighborhoods. The goal would be a gradual expansion of integrated education in communities where middle-class families with children could settle.

8) Revising State and Federal Housing Regulations. The experience of the Michigan State Housing Development Authority, and of HUD-funded mobility programs in Chicago and Baltimore, shows that state and federal regulations and funding priorities can assist the development of integrated housing. Organizations such as the Council of State Housing Finance Agencies and the Education Commission of the States could play a very useful role in identifying positive experiences and suggesting improved policies to state agencies. At a time when the State of Missouri is under a federal court order to develop both school and housing desegregation plans for its largest metropolitan area, and when the issues are being raised in litigation elsewhere, such work could be valuable to responsible officials and to the courts.

HUD has begun to review some of its regulations with the school problem in mind, but much more could be done to improve federal rules. In early 1981, HUD issued site-selection policies for subsidized housing that called, in a very general way, for consideration of impacts on court-ordered school desegregation plans. The positive experiences of Charlotte and Louisville, as well as the commitments made by HUD in the St. Louis case and by the Justice Department in the Chicago school case, could be the basis for developing a new regulatory framework for housing decisions in communities with desegregated schools. The evidence is clear that, in the absence of such a framework, federal housing funds are likely to support actions that undermine the goal of the federal courts in the school orders.

9) Litigation. The history of civil rights enforcement is full of examples of reasonable integration proposals rejected or ignored by responsible elected or appointed officials. An important tool in an overall urban integration strategy is a legal approach that can help provide either an important incentive for voluntary local action or an effective ultimate sanction if government authorities refuse to act.

In the near future there is likely to be very little path-finding Justice Department litigation against urban segregation. Nevertheless, private nonprofit agencies, civil rights organizations, and academic researchers should be encouraged to devise new legal theories under state and federal law. They should also investigate the impact of historic school and housing segregation on the racial patterns of major metropolitan areas. Given the great political sensitivity of these issues and the considerable cost of the necessary work, this need is likely to be met only through private foundations.

10) Integration Subsidies. White flight from the cities has been subsidized on a vast scale by a complex system of tax expenditures, depreciation allowances, redlining and appraisal policies tilted toward new development, freeway construction, and an array of other costly policies. Leaders of the U.S. Commission on Civil Rights and of various housing-integration organizations have often discussed, in general terms, the desirability of using subsidies or incentives to support integration.

The issue is a sensitive one, easily misunderstood, but it deserves exploration. Integration incentives would not be "hardship pay" for living with people from another racial background. They would recognize that in the past we have offered large subsidies for moves that have increased segregation—subsidies that went in disproportionate amounts to whites leaving cities. Thus, we need to counter the impact of this process by creating fiscal incentives for moves that support the national goal of open housing and ease the desegregation burden on school districts.

The Suburban Action Institute's report, *Housing Choice*, describes dozens of state and local programs that now provide direct or indirect subsidies to lower housing costs for some buyers and renters. These programs rarely address directly the goal of integration; they simply attempt to make housing available for low-income families. With a recruitment and counseling component, they could serve both purposes. A great many communities—both cities and suburbs—are subsidizing home ownership across a broad economic spectrum through mortgage-bond programs. These tax-exempt bonds substantially lower the cost of home purchase but involve large losses to the federal treasury. The money is usually simply injected into the mortgage market with few restrictions. Giving preference to families and to moves that contribute to integration could be a powerful incentive.

A few small, private efforts, such as M-REIT, the Fund for an OPEN Society, and Westchester Residential Opportunities, have intentionally invested funds in integrated rental housing. They have also provided revolving funds to help minority families purchasing their first home to move into a white area. We now have a significant amount of experience showing the workability of these approaches. Commitments by local businesses, foundations, and financial institutions to encourage pioneers—who are initiating integration in neighborhoods where almost all the residents are of another race—could be a positive contribution. Far fewer minority than white families have a substantial equity in their homes, and many need some aid in first-home purchase if they are to have any chance to live outside a segregated community.

A government with a strong market orientation might well consider incentives as well as sanctions in its fair-housing strategy. Realtors often discriminate because they may lose business and money if they alienate local whites by selling a house to a black or Hispanic. They see nothing tangible to gain by observing the law. If the government does not wish to increase its sanctions, making discrimination much more costly, perhaps it should encourage experiments that offer a financial gain for compliance. Would it make a difference, for example, if the agent who sold the first house in a neighborhood to someone of a different race received a $1,000 bonus? (In the Gautreaux experiment, $1,000 was the approximate cost of moving a family to assisted rental housing in the Chicago suburbs; it is also the cost of a single year's busing for the children in a large family.)

There are many other forms of direct and indirect subsidies. At present, very little information is available on their chances of success. Given the weakness of current fair-housing law, the defeat of the 1980 fair-housing enforcement bill, and the commonplace use of subsidies in the housing market, government and private agencies should encourage experimentation and evaluation. Perhaps some of the techniques that helped to intensify the problem can be employed to mitigate its effects.

References

[1] A 1980 Gallup Poll showed, for instance, that 68 per cent of whites already believed that local blacks were treated the same as whites, and 75 per cent of whites believed that the quality of life for blacks had improved in the past decade. *(Gallup Opinion Index,* June 1980, pp. 9, 10.)

[2] A Gallup Poll on alternatives to busing showed considerable support for housing solutions. *(Gallup Opinion Index,* December 1973, p. 25.) An in-depth survey of blacks and whites in metropolitan Columbus, Ohio, in 1979 showed widespread support for housing alternatives among both whites and blacks. (David Larson and Gerald G. Newborg, *Franklin County Fair Housing Research Study,* report to Franklin County Commissioners. Columbus: Archival Systems, 1979.)

[3] Interview with Dominic Schuler, Director Housing Division, HUD Area Office, Louisville, Ky., December 7, 1979.

[4] Gerald E. Von Stroh, *Denver Metropolitan Areas Residential Migration,* Denver Urban Observatory, 1975; Alice Woldt, *Real Estate Marketing Practices and Residential Segregation,* report in National Institute of Education series "Schools and Neighborhoods Research Study" prepared for City of Seattle and Seattle Public Schools; Oliver Quayle and Company, survey for Wilmington Department of Planning and Development, 1974, p. 107; Larson and Newborg; Willis Hawley and John McConahay, "Attitudes of Louisville and Jefferson County Citizens Toward Busing for Public School Desegregation," report based on Louis Harris survey of metropolitan Louisville, 1976.

[5] Kale Williams, Donald DeMarco, and Dudley Onderdonk, "Affirmative Action in Housing—An Emerging Public Issue," Governors State University Institute for Public Policy and Administration Research Report, 1980; Joyce Gemperlein, "A Nice Place, A Proud Place: Willingboro," *Philadelphia Inquirer,* August 28, 1980; Toby Sachs, *The Oak Park Experience,* Northeastern Illinois Planning Commission Staff Paper, November 1976.

[6] The pattern of inaction was clear in all city governments studied except those of Charlotte, N.C., and Ann Arbor, Mich.

[7] Interview with Duane W. Krohnke, Counsel for Minneapolis Public Schools, January 11, 1980.

[8] Interview with Galen Martin, December 7, 1979.

[9] *Hart* v *Community School Bd., Dist. No. 21,* 383 F. Supp. 769 (E.D. N. Y., 1974), 383 F. Supp. 769 (E.D. N.Y. 1974).

[10] *Liddell* v *Board of Education of the City of St. Louis,* No. 72-100-G (4) (E.D., Mo., May 21, 1980).

[11] *Evans* v *Buchanan,* 393 F. Supp. 428 (D. Del., 1975), 416 F. Supp. 328 (D. Del., 1976), *aff'd,* 423 U.S. 963 (1975); *United States* v *Board of School Commissioners of the City of Indianapolis,* No. 78-1800 (7th Cir., April 29, 1980).

[12] This was a basic argument of the school district in the St. Louis, Mo. case, and it was initially accepted by the U.S. District Court, only to be reversed by the Court of Appeals.

[13] *Newburg Area Council, Inc.,* v *Gordon,* 521 F. 2d 578 (5th Cir., 1975).

[14] The exemptions are described in John A. Finger, Jr., "Policy Requirements for Successful Big-City Desegregation," in Daniel U. Levine and Robert J. Havighurst (eds.), *The Future of Big City Schools* (Berkeley: McCutchan, 1977), p. 213.

[15] Interviews with Howard Merriman and Calvin Smith, Columbus Public Schools, August 27, 1980.

[16] Bernard Gifford, Report to the Honorable Judge Paul Egly, Superior Court of California for the County of Los Angeles, *Crawford* v *Board of Education of the City of Los Angeles,* November 14, 1978.

[17] St. Louis Board of Education, "Desegregation Plan of the Board of Education of the City of St. Louis," submitted to U.S. District Court for the Eastern District of Missouri, May 2, 1980, p. 10; *Liddell* order, May 21, 1980. The exemption was subsequently extended at the request of the Board of Education.

[18] *Louisville Times,* May 28, 1980.

[19] Ibid.

[20] Galen Martin, Kentucky Human Rights Commission, Memorandum, June 19, 1980.

[21] Interviews with James Cordery, Zane Griffin, and Kathi Whalen, Housing Authority and Community Development Agency of Jefferson County; interview with Assistant Superintendent Frank Rapley, Jefferson County Public Schools.

[22] Kentucky Commission on Human Rights, *Discriminatory Practices Determine Housing Choices in Fayette and Jefferson* (Frankfort, Ky ., 1978), pp. 1, 5.

[23] The case, brought by Julius Chambers of the NAACP Legal Defense Fund, ended with an out-of-court settlement providing better policies for the future.

[24] *Hernandez* v *Special School Dist. No. 1, Minneapolis,* No. 4-78-Civ. 369, Memorandum Order, August 24, 1978.

[25] Interview with David Bennett, Deputy Superintendent, Milwaukee Public Schools, November 15, 1979. Bennett reported that there had been no discussion within the school district of the possibility of special treatment for the schools in integrated neighborhoods.

[26] Lois Quinn, "Relationships Between School Desegregation and Government Housing Programs: A Milwaukee Case Study," draft report to National Institute of Education, November 1980, p. 6.

[27] Los Angeles School Monitoring Commission, Thirteenth Report, submitted to Superior Court, County of Los Angeles.

[28] Quinn, p. 6.

[29] Ibid., p. 4, and Chapter 4.

[30] The change in Hidden Valley School and the related decisions are described in the *Charlotte Observer*, September 23, 1971; June 15, 1973; February 1, 1974. By 1979 the school had the highest black segregation level in metropolitan Charlotte. (*Charlotte News*, October 24, 1979, p. 1A.)

[31] Interviews with Champaign Mayor Joan Severns, Champaign Planning Department Director Bette McKown, and John Demet of the Champaign County Regional Planning Commission, March 1980. (These interviews were conducted by Marilyn Cohen, research associate on this project.) Reports of the housing plans were found in *Champaign-Urbana News-Gazette*, June 8, 1980.

[32] *Liddell* v *Board of Education*, 491 F. Supp. 351 (E.D. Mo., 1980).

[33] St. Louis Board of Education, *Desegregation Plan*, with amendments.

[34] St. Louis Community Development Agency and St. Louis Board of Education, "St. Louis Metropolitan Housing Plan," submitted to U.S. District Court, St. Louis, November 28, 1980; U.S. Department of Justice, "Plan Submitted Pursuant to Paragraph 12 (d) of This Court's Order of May 21, 1980," November 21, 1980.

[35] Karl Taeuber and Alma Taeuber, *Negroes in Cities* (New York: Atheneum, 1969), pp. 99-125.

[36] Rose Helper, *Racial Policies and Practices of Real Estate Brokers* (Minneapolis: University of Minnesota Press, 1969); Diana M. Pearce, "Black, White and Many Shades of Gray: Real Estate Brokers and their Racial Practices," unpublished Ph.D. dissertation, 1976.

[37] Diana Pearce, "Breaking Down Barriers: New Evidence on the Impact of Metropolitan School Desegregation on Housing Patterns," report submitted to National Institute of Education, November 1980.

[38] Alice Woldt, *Real Estate Marketing Practices and Residential Segregation*, Seattle Schools and Neighborhoods Research Study, January 1978, p. 17.

[39] Gary Orfield, *Desegregation in the Cities: The Trends and The Policy Choices*, staff report, U.S. Senate Committee on Human Resources, 95th Cong., 1st sess., 1977, pp. 23-24.

[40] Regional Plan Association, *Regional Plan News*, "Segregation and Opportunity in the Region's Housing," July 1979, p. 23.

[41] U.S. Department of Housing and Urban Development, *Measuring Racial Discrimination in American Housing Markets*, 1979.

[42] *Congressional Record*, December 9, 1980, pp. S15850–S15860. Supporters fell six votes short of the 60 needed to cut off a Senate filibuster.

[43] Peter W. Colby and Larry McClellan, "Can Public Policy Decisions Prevent Suburban Racial Resegregation?" paper delivered at the 1980 Annual Meeting of Midwest Political Science Association, Chicago, April 20-22, 1980.

[44] Claudia Levy, "Erasing Baltimore's Redlining," *Washington Post*, April 25, 1976.

[45] Richard L. Taub and D. Carth Taylor, "Crime and Urban Development," draft report for Crime and Neighborhoods Project at the National Opinion Research Center, University of Chicago, May 1980, p. 79.

[46] Ibid., pp. 31-32.

[47] A. Richard Gloor, "Integration: A Success Story," *Real Estate Today*, April 1976, pp. 50-53.

[48] Diana Pearce made such tests in 1978.

[49] U.S. Commission on Civil Rights, *Home Ownership for Low Income Families*, 1971; Richard Fleischer, "Subsidized Housing and American Cities: An Evaluation of the Site Selection and Occupancy Selection of Federally Subsidized Housing," unpublished Ph.D. dissertation, 1980. Gary Orfield and Paul Fischer, *Housing and School Integration in Three Metropolitan Areas: A Policy Analysis of Denver, Columbus, and Phoenix*, submitted to January 13, 1981.

[50] Taeuber and Taeuber, pp. 99-125; Otis Dudley Duncan and Beverly Duncan, *The Negro Population of Chicago* (Chicago: University of Chicago Press, 1957); Helper, *Racial Policies and Practices of Real Estate Brokers;* Harvey Luskin Molotch, *Managed Integration: Dilemmas of Doing Good in The City* (Berkeley and Los Angeles: University of California Press, 1972).

[51] Henry Jay Becker, "Racially Integrated Neighborhoods: Do White Families Move In? Which Ones?" Center for Social Organization of Schools, Johns Hopkins University, Rept. No. 287, November 1979, pp. 18-26, 33-37.

[52] Taub and Taylor, p. 62.

[53] The Exchange Congress, headquartered in Oak Park, Ill., held its 4th annual meeting in October 1980 in Oak Park.

[54] Interview with Teaneck Superintendent Aubry Sher, November 28, 1979.

[55] Interview with Lucille K. Anderson, Director, Shaker Heights Housing Office, May 30, 1980.

[56] The problem, at Old Mill Lane School, is closely related to the rapid conversion of a large apartment complex to housing for black tenants in Section 8 housing. (Interview with John Parres, New Castle Co. Public Schools, January 17, 1980.)

[57] Sixty-one per cent of white parents said they would not be willing to have their children transported even if they "were convinced that your

child would get a better education than he or she now is getting in your neighborhood school." (Letter from Oscar J. Kaplan, Research Director, San Diego Poll to San Diego School Supt. Thomas L. Goodman, May 2, 1978.)

[58] Nancy Burton and Dick Birnbaum, *Minority Population in the Seattle Area*, "Seattle Schools and Neighborhoods Study," October 1977, p. 112; Gary Christophersen and Michael Wills, *Metropolitan Mobility Survey*, "Seattle Schools and Neighborhoods Study," July 15, 1977, p. 5.

[59] Marie Fielder (ed.), *School Resegregation: Residential and School Process*, report submitted to National Institute of Education by Bay Area Learning Center—Berkeley Section, the Berkeley Unified School District and the Office of Project Planning, Development and Evaluation, Berkeley, Calif., August 1977, p. 101.

[60] Fielder, p. 102.

[61] Fielder, pp. 103, 158.

[62] *Education U.S.A.*, July 25, 1977; Wendell Rawls, "Atlanta Does Its Homework on School's Value," *St. Louis Post-Dispatch*, March 24, 1980; Lawrence H. Hall, "Englewood Hunts White Students," *Newark Star-Ledger,* August 28, 1977; Marjorie Kaplan, "Freeport Tackles White Flight," *Newsday*, May 6, 1979.

[63] Figures on racial change and school enrollment in the Austin neighborhood of Chicago are reported in Carole Goodwin, *The Oak Park Strategy* (Chicago: University of Chicago Press, 1979), pp. 84-86; Becker, p. 13.

[64] J. Dennis Lord and John C. Catau, "School Desegregation Policy and Intra-School District Migration," *Social Science Quarterly* (March 1977), pp. 784-796; Diana Pearce, "Breaking Down Barriers," p. 50.

[65] Eugene C. Royster and Associates, *Study of the Emergency School Aid Magnet School Program* (Cambridge: Abt Associates, 1979).

[66] Los Angeles School Monitoring Committee, Sixth Report, Seventh Report, Thirteenth Report, submitted to Superior Court for State of California for County of Los Angeles.

[67] Massachusetts and Wisconsin have state legislation that funds voluntary interdistrict transfers.

[68] Data provided by Illinois Office of Education; for a discussion see Gary Orfield, "Voluntary Desegregation in Chicago," a report to the State Superintendent of Education, February 26, 1979.

[69] Personal communication with author.

[70] The Village of Bellwood continually objected to this policy without success, pointing out that, in a school district changing racial composition ½ per cent a month, a policy limited to that single district made little sense. Letter from Bellwood Mayor Sigel Davis to State Superintendent Joseph Cronin, February 11, 1980.

[71] Goodwin, *The Oak Park Stategy;* Reginald G. Damerell, *Triumph in a White Suburb* (New York: Apollo Editions, 1968); Peter Rossi and Robert

Dentler, *The Politics of Urban Renewal* (New York: The Free Press, 1961); Julia Abrahamson, *A Neighborhood Finds Itself* (New York: Harper and Row, 1959).

[72] Garlie A. Forehand, Marjorie Ragosta, and Donald A. Rock, *Conditions and Processes of Effective School Desegregation* (Princeton: Educational Testing Service, 1976); Gary Orfield, "How to Make Desegregation Work: The Adaptation of Schools to their Newly-Integrated Student Bodies," *Law and Contemporary Problems,* vol. 39 (Spring 1975), pp. 314-340.

[73] The schools involved were Gage Park High and Morgan Park High.

[74] In 1975 an initial quota of 42 per cent black students was set for Gage Park High School; in 1976 a 50 per cent black quota was set for Morgan Park High School. After five years Gage Park remained 40 per cent white, and after four years Morgan Park remained 42 per cent white. Neither school had changed in the rapid fashion characteristic of Chicago.

[75] The case was accepted for review by the U.S. Supreme Court but the Chicago school board mooted the dispute when it withdrew the plan in the fall of 1980 as part of the process of preparing a citywide desegregation plan.

[76] Patricia Camp, "25,000 Displaced Here in 5 Years," *Washington Post,* February 1, 1980.

[77] John E. Jacob, "The District: White In-migration, Black Exodus," *Washington Post,* May 2, 1979.

[78] A state court decision in California recognizes the possibility that rental policies discriminating against children could harm school integration. "Ban on Children in Rental Housing Upset on Coast," *New York Times,* January 3, 1979, reporting on appellate decision in *Marina Point, Ltd.* v *Wolfson.*

[79] This has been a basic feature of St. Louis plans for use of the HUD Section 8 New Construction program.

[80] Chris Ganley, ed., *Catholic Schools in America* (Denver: Curriculum Information Center, 1975); Orfield, *Must We Bus?* (Washington: Brookings Institution, 1978), pp. 60-61.

[81] Taub and Taylor, pp. 62-64.

[82] Becker, "Racially Integrated Neighborhoods," pp. 33-37.

[83] Robert L. Green and Associates, *Metropolitan School Desegregation in New Castle County, Delaware,* Report to Rockefeller Foundation, June 1980, pp. 1-18.

[84] Steve Goldberg, "Some Pupils Who Fled Return to Public School," *Wilmington News Journal,* March 9, 1980, p. B-1. New Castle County School District, "Enrollment Update as of January 4, 1980."

[85] Interviews with Winston E. Cleland, Stewart Harrison, and John Parres, New Castle County Public Schools, January 17, 1980.

[86] A smaller, far less selective school was subsequently authorized and

will open in the fall of 1981. Adjoining the Howard University campus, it will be unlikely to attract whites.

[87] Fielder, *School Resegregation*, pp. 101-102; Christophersen and Willis, *Metropolitan Mobility Survey*, p. 5.

[88] Diane Brockett, "Change Lifts School Hopes," *Washington Star*, March 29, 1974; Lee Daniels, "Capitol Hill School is Something Special," *Washington Post*, September 29, 1975.

[89] Taub and Taylor, pp. 2-3.

[90] Ibid., p. 50.

[91] Ibid., pp. 26, 39, 41, 63.

[92] Ibid., p. 64.

[93] Technical Assistance Committee on the Chicago Desegregation Plan, *Integration in Chicago*, Report to Illinois State Board of Education, May 1978, p. 29; enrollment statistics from Illinois Office of Education.

[94] A 1978 Harris Survey found that only 23 per cent of whites thought that blacks were discriminated against in the housing market. (Louis Harris and Associates, "A Study of Attitudes Toward Racial and Religious Minorities and Toward Women," report to the National Conference of Christians and Jews, November 1978, p. 5.

[95] Ibid., p. 13. Only 7 per cent of blacks favor "separation of the races." Thomas Pettigrew, "Attitudes on Race and Housing: A Social-Psychological View," in Hawley and Rock (eds.), *Segregation in Residential Areas* (Washington: National Academy of Sciences, 1973), pp. 21-48.

[96] Albert I. Hermalin and Reynolds Farley, "The Potential for Residential Integration in Cities and Suburbs," *American Sociological Review*, vol. 38 (October 1973), pp. 597-601.

[97] The bill was first weakened and then defeated in the session of Congress that followed the election of Ronald Reagan.

[98] This was done by the Ohio legislature as part of a series of actions intended to foster alternatives to busing. (Peggy Siegel, "The Three R's: Race, Roll Calls & Real Estate: How the Ohio Legislature Enacted Fair Housing/Desegregation Reforms in 1979," *Progress* (Summer/Fall 1979), pp. 1-6.

[99] Ibid.

[100] Interview with Frank Williams, President, Southside Branch, Chicago NAACP.

[101] This is true, for example, of the Equal Employment Opportunities Commission.

[102] Judith A. Haig, "A Study to Determine the Extent of Compliance Among Developers/Sponsors with Equal Housing Advertising Guidelines and Affirmative Marketing Regulations," p. 39. (This study reported a low level of knowledge of fair housing in 15 cities.) A recent survey of blacks in metropolitan Columbus, Ohio, found that, although there was a strong preference for integrated housing, almost half the blacks believed it was still legal for whites to discriminate. (David Larson

and Gerald G. Newborg, *Franklin County Fair Housing Research Study*, report to Franklin County Commissioners [Columbus: Archival Systems, 1979], pp. 42, 60.)

[103] Nathaniel Sheppard, Jr., "East St. Louis Mayor Seeks to Reverse Decaying City's Fortunes," *New York Times*, December 19, 1980.

[104] Interview with Kermit Lind, Executive Director, Cuyahoga Plan, May 30, 1980.

[105] Letter from Galen Martin, Executive Director, Kentucky Commission on Human Rights to Assistant Attorney General Drew Days III, December 15, 1978.

[106] *Hills* v *Gautreaux*, 425 U.S. 284 (1976).

[107] Martin Meyerson and Edward C. Banfield, *Politics, Planning and the Public Interest: The Case of Public Housing in Chicago* (Glencoe, Ill., The Free Press, 1955).

[108] Division of Policy Studies, U.S. Department of Housing and Urban Development, *The Gautreaux Housing Demonstration: An Evaluation of its Impact on Participating Households*, 1979, p. 76.

[109] Ibid., pp. 4, 36.

[110] Ibid., pp. 9, 10.

[111] Ibid., p. 105.

[112] Ibid., pp. 113, 132.

[113] Ibid., p. 135.

[114] Ibid., p. 67.

[115] Letter from Kale Williams, Executive Director, Leadership Council of Metropolitan Open Communities, to Friends of Open Housing, December 1980.

[116] "Denver Schools and Housing," in Gary Orfield and Paul Fischer, *Housing and School Integration in Three Metropolitan Areas: A Policy Analysis of Denver, Columbus, and Phoenix*, submitted to U.S. Dept. of Housing and Urban Development, January 13, 1981, pp. 21-23.

[117] Minneapolis Public Schools, "Public-Personnel Sight Count," October 1979; Committee on School Desegregation, Citizens League, "Citizens League Report," December 12, 1979; A. Philip Andrus and Associates, *Seattle* (Cambridge, Mass.: Ballinger, 1976); Carol S. Baron, *1977–78 Racial Distribution of Students and Staff* (Seattle Public Schools, Rept. 77-27, December 10, 1977).

[118] U.S. Commission on Civil Rights, *Home Ownership for Lower Income Families*, 1971.

[119] Interviews with Chuck Ballentine, Senior Planner, and Nancy Reeves, Director, Housing Division, Metropolitan Council, January 11, 1980; telephone interview with Jay Haavik, Puget Sound Council of Governments, January 9, 1980.

[120] Haavik interview; interview with Ronald L. Oldham, Director of Resident Services, Seattle Housing Authority, January 8, 1980.

[121] Ballentine and Reeves interviews.

[122] Richard Fleisher, "Subsidized Housing and Residential Segregation in American Cities: An Evaluation of the Site Selection and Occupancy of Federally Subsidized Housing," unpublished Ph.D. dissertation, Department of Political Science, University of Illinois at Urbana-Champaign, 1979.

[123] Ibid., chapter 6; for results, including the impact of the Section 8 existing rent subsidy program, see Orfield and Fischer; for an analysis of the built-in inadequacies of HUD's civil rights data system, see: G. Orfield, "Measuring Equity Requires Measuring Integration," paper prepared for HUD Office of Fair Housing and Equal Opportunity, May 1981.

[124] Suburban Action Institute, *Housing Choice: A Handbook for Suburban Officials* (New York: Suburban Action Institute, 1980), pp. 134-137. There are similar programs in several other communities.

[125] Ibid., pp. 138-139.

[126] Sam Kaplan, "Actions Lead to Affordable Units," *Los Angeles Times*, July 13, 1980.

[127] Gideon Golany (ed.), *Strategy for New Community Development in the United States* (Stroudsburg, Pa.: Dowden, Hutchinson & Ross, 1975), pp. 61-68; Carlos C. Campbell, *New Towns: Another Way to Live* (Reston: Reston Publishing, 1976), pp. 89-115.

[128] City of Ann Arbor, "Housing Assistance Plan Entitlement Application, Fifth Year, Fiscal Year 1980," p. iv.

[129] City of Ann Arbor, Community Development Office, "Parkway Meadows, Rent Up Survey," July 1980.

[130] Michigan State Housing Development Authority, *Annual Report*, 1978, p. 13.

[131] Michigan State Housing Development Authority, p. 3.

[132] Jerry Shinn, "Housing Plans Would End Lip Service to Integration," *Charlotte Observer*, February 19, 1975.

[133] Interviews with Jack Bullard, Community Relations Commission, November 8, 1980; Ray Wheeling, Director, Charlotte Housing Authority, November 8, 1980; Donald Carroll, Jr., Charlotte City Council, November 8, 1979.

[134] Interview with Fred Bryant, Charlotte-Mecklenburg Planning Commission, November 8, 1979.